RELISH YOUR RETIRE[

501 FUN, INSIGHTFUL AND SIMPLE IDEA
BLISSFUL RETIRED LIFE FOR WOME

FLORANCE PHILIP

Dedicated to the precious lady reading this page now. Yes, this book is dedicated to you. Hope you enjoy reading this book.

CONTENTS

ACKNOWLEDGMENTS

I start by thanking my Almighty God.

Thank you to my loving husband and my two little ones for their precious love and support. Thanks to my mom, who reads every word I write and whose retirement inspired me to write this book. Thanks to my dad for all his love, wisdom, and guidance. Thanks to my loving sister, aunt, close family members, and dearest friends for all the love, support, good words, and encouragement. Having an idea and turning it into a book is as hard as it sounds. The experience is both rewarding and challenging. I especially thank everyone who helped make this happen. You all have a special place in my heart

INTRODUCTION

Are you ready to become excited (*once again*) about retirement? To look upon this phase with renewed hope and enthusiasm? What could be more empowering and fun than discovering who you truly are, separate from your career, family, and community? It is time once again to think about who you want to be when you grow up, only this time - **there are no limitations!**

———

Rose was the chief office coordinator of an international airline, a position she had held for over twenty years. As she approached her twilight years, colleagues eagerly asked her when she would retire.

However, Rose's feelings about retirement were closer to dread than hopeful anticipation. She loved her job, was passionate about her work and excelled in her career. Every day was a flurry of activities that brought exciting challenges and opportunities to work alongside some fantastic people. For nine hours a day, five days a week, Rose relished being a respected and valued member of her team.

When she turned sixty, retirement became a reality. On her last day, surrounded by coworkers who gushed over her previous successes and wished her well in her new journey, Rose was struck by how much her life was about to change. She was doubtful — was retirement a blessing or a curse? Rose was overjoyed at not having to apply for approval for holidays and at being able to spend more time with her kids and grandkids. But what would she do with her new 45-plus hours of freedom each week? How would she put her skills to good use? How would she fill the void in her social life left by her colleagues? Rose's retirement was the epitome of bittersweet. She pondered: was the price of her freedom her identity and value?

Retirement. It's a phase of life that almost everyone dreams about at one point or another, so it shouldn't come as a surprise when it finally arrives. But then why does it blindside so many of us, much like Rose?

A common phrase among retirees, young, old, or in between, is "Retirement isn't what I thought it would be." And we have honestly had a lot of time to think about what it would look and feel like, haven't we? From the time we enter the workforce as young adults, retirement has been with us. In the beginning, it may seem far off, unattainable even, as you slowly begin contributing to your retirement fund. Though from that first deposit, we plan and envision what we will do with our lives once it's no longer dictated by work. The idea was slowly growing, like the savings in our retirement accounts. Even for those of us who love our jobs and thrive in our careers, retirement will eventually become a reality. Retirement is not just for the office goers; stay-at-home mothers will face a day when their children have grown and left the nest, and they are essentially in retirement. One way or another, retirement is coming for all of us.

Then suddenly, your colleagues wish you well, your last paycheck is issued, and you leave your office, classroom, or business for the last time. You've done the hard work, saved up enough to get by, and are now headed out on a new adventure. It should be exciting and celebratory; after all, it's the day you've likely waited nearly thirty years for. Then why do so many of us women use other adjectives to describe what should be one of life's happiest milestones? Words like daunting, scary, even depressing.

You are not alone if you're feeling a bit adrift after retirement. Scouring the internet and other resources, you will find a great deal about how to plan and save for retirement but a shortage of information on anything not related to the financial side of retiring. No, you are not an outlier for feeling the way you do. Millions of individuals struggle to transition into retirement effortlessly and blissfully. Sadly, there isn't a lot out there regarding the emotional and mental aspects of retiring. It is astounding to think about how big a transition retirement truly is.

As much as we love to believe that our job doesn't define us, it is an integral part of who we are as a person for most of our adult life. It gives us purpose each day, a measurable task, and a way to visualize progress towards a goal. Our job offers us a chance to interact with others, leave our homes, and hopefully form some great friendships with our peers. When that is suddenly stripped away, all the preparation in the world might not be enough to keep you from feeling lonely and lost. The transition can be confusing, to say the least. Emotions of happiness and excitement mingle with less pleasant feelings of uncertainty and boredom.

A friend of mine recently announced her retirement. I was eager to congratulate her on such an enormous accomplishment. But as soon as the sentiment left my lips, I could tell it was not what she wanted to hear. She confessed it was true; she was excited not to wake up early anymore or operate her life around someone else's schedule, but she was wary about her impending retirement life. At the time, my friend was divorced and lived comfortably with the companionship of her dog. Her coworkers provided daily social interaction deeper than just a "hello" with the market cashier. She had two children, I argued, that would surely love to see her more often. She responded that one son lived out of state and the other, who had a child of his own, led a busy life. They were in their prime, as you might say, with a schedule bursting with jobs, school, and extracurriculars, leaving little extra time for visits from grandma. Her planned holiday with a friend had been canceled, to top it all off. She was now faced with a wide-open calendar, but that freedom didn't sound as inviting as it once had. Instead of wanting to celebrate, she looked as if all she wanted to do was cry. She admitted reluctantly that it felt like she was in mourning, suffering the loss of her job, friends, and identity so tightly interwoven with her career title.

I remember thinking I wished I had something mean-ingful to say or a thoughtful piece of advice that I could give her. I was young and still relatively unfamiliar with retirement, choosing to ignore the fact that along with the congratulations and cards came a life-altering tran-sition. At the moment, all I could do was listen and acknowledge her feelings.

Whether you are retired, are approaching retirement, or know someone for whom retirement is a reality (arguably all of us), I believe we shouldn't have to look at this momentous life event with trepidation. Sure, we can take off the rose-colored glasses that led us to believe retirement is all holidays and social clubs, but this doesn't mean their absence leaves us with a bleak outlook on living, spending the rest of our days without purpose or passion.

And that's what retirement is all about: finding what you are passionate about. It's an opportunity to get reacquainted with yourself. Or, if you desire, to rein-vent yourself. There's no denying that the path to a happy retirement won't always be smooth or straight, but there's a joy that you get to dictate your own jour-ney. For once, no one is watching the clock, hustling you along, or marking your progress. You'll discover that retirement is the journey, not the destination.

Retirement is a transition, so treat it like one. Slowly, gradually; give yourself grace as you adjust to finding your renewed purpose, or purposes, in life.

This book is not meant to be your guide. After all, you are now the master of your journey. Instead, treat this book as a roadmap filled with points of interest, sights to pause and relish life, insightful ideas to ponder, and helpful tips for making your new journey more manageable and smoother. There are fun and thoughtful ideas you can try every other day, weekly, on weekends, or whenever you please. At the end of each chapter, there are insightful and joyful activities related to that chapter. We discuss friendly insights on renewing your zest for life, reigniting those passions and dreams you have long let smolder, and we affirm that what you feel is valid.

Who would have thought you would need guidance on living, after living half a century? It's safe to say I put myself firmly in the group that thought we had everything perfectly planned. But don't misjudge retirement; it's as significant a life change as getting married or having a baby. Unfortunately, we don't get to slowly enjoy the unfolding of this phase as we do with the blooming of love or the growth of a baby. Nevertheless, the emotions are the same, exciting and joyous, but also foreign and new. As you shift and grapple with your new reality, prepare to put in some work in the form of self-examination. This self-work isn't selfish, and for a time, personal development should be your priority. I hope this handy guide can give you the tips and tricks to help you age dynamically and enjoy your retirement.

1

CLEARING THE IDENTITY CRISIS HURDLE

*D*o you remember those carefree days you experienced as a child? Where your biggest worry was if your mom had remembered to pack you a treat in your lunch or if your soccer team would win the weekend match? Whether or not you could attend your best friend's birthday party this weekend, which gorgeous outfit you would wear to wow your girlfriends, wondering what presents you would get for your birthday or this Christmas, or if mom and dad would take you to see that new movie or circus show you desperately wanted to see? There were no looming deadlines, timecards to punch, or bosses dictating where you had to be and when, as long as you made it home in time for dinner. Life was simple. You lived boldly and dreamed big, aspiring to one day be an astronaut, a doctor, a teacher, or maybe something a little closer to home, like a CEO. Until one day, people stopped asking you what you wanted to be when you grew up because you were grown up, with a career and maybe a family.

For many of us, somewhere along the way, our dreams turned into our jobs, and our jobs slowly evolved into our identities. It is probably safe to hazard a guess that you have longed for the days of childhood freedom on more than one occasion in your adult working life. Maybe you were stressed over a project timeline, working under an unfriendly boss, struggling to get out of bed on a cold Monday morning, or perhaps just beleaguered at the thought of another work week. Yet, for all our daydreaming about what we would do with that free life, if suddenly that fantasy becomes a reality and we are handed our freedom, our life comes to a sudden halt.

A day off from work is relaxing, a week is liberating, but an eternity? Terrifying. One word seals your fate, sometimes by force but often by choice—'retirement'. Why is retirement so frightening? Often, even those who love their jobs look forward to the weekend. Then why is the promise of unlimited weekends enough to have us hiding under the covers, unwilling to face the world?

The answer is simple, but the understanding that follows is complex. For a large percentage of working adults, their career and their identity are indistinguishably intertwined. Think about meeting someone new. What is often one of the first questions you ask? "What do you do for work?" Our job is a massive part of who we are. Many of us spend forty hours a week (or more) at our jobs; that's at least eight hours out of a twenty-four-hour day, which is one-third of a day, where the other two-thirds are divided between sleeping and keeping up with life's other demands. Work consumes a third of our day. It isn't hard to see why work can shape who we are. Our coworkers become our friends, our office — our home away from home, and our employer's mission becomes our mission. If someone were to ask you, "Who are you?" you might say a parent or name your religion, but your answer will undoubtedly include your role at work. Who are you? A teacher. A flight attendant. An accountant. A real estate agent. A lawyer. A business owner. An office assistant. For the majority of your adult life, your life is focused on your career.

Then, be it planned or unforeseen, retirement suddenly strips part of your identity away. Who are you? What do you do? What fills one-third of your day? In the blink of an eye, you're at the end. It seems as if you have peaked. Everything you have worked so hard for, starting in grade school and continuing through promotions and career changes, culminates with a pension, a pat on the back, and a perpetually blank calendar. We almost always have something to look forward to until, it seems, we retire.

"Often when you think you're at the end of something, you're at the beginning of something else."

— FRED ROGERS

I rest my case on why retirement can be so alarming; it's a significant life shift. Now, it's time to embrace the challenge. The realization that "who you are" can exist entirely separate from "'what you do for work'" is the beginning of your journey to a fulfilled retirement. Your career doesn't have the power to take away who you really are, your true identity. It never has, it never will. Your job does not define you now. It does not matter if your job resulted from expectations imposed upon you by your family or friends or if you were extremely passionate about your work.

Your identity might require a slight reshaping and refocusing, but it is still there in its essence. Rediscovering who you are is one of the most enjoyable parts of retirement. It is most definitely work, but what work could be more fulfilling than rejuvenating or maybe recreating who you indeed are? And no, your age is not a factor in reinventing yourself.

The definition of retirement in the dictionary is "the action or fact of leaving one's job and ceasing to work." It doesn't say anything about ceasing to live. You're free from obligations and expectations, allowing you to embark on a journey of self-introspection. All this sounds wonderful, but in reality, many of us aren't ready to begin putting in the effort on day one of our retirement — the majority of individuals approaching retirement pass through five distinct stages of emotions.

A lack of progression through these stages can make awareness and acceptance difficult. Suppose you're having a hard time coping with your transition into the new chapter in your life of "senior-dom." In that case, I encourage you to look at the following phases and try to determine which one accurately describes you. Then, you look forward and prepare yourself for the shedding of your career identity and the transition into a significantly meaningful new life.

THE FIVE STAGES OF RETIREMENT

Stage One: The Planning

Chances are, you completed some sort of retirement planning. It likely was financial, which was undoubtedly a good thing to do. However, don't overlook planning for the emotional component of exiting your job. It is a considerable change in your life. Acknowledging the profound shift and its effects on your well-being is vital.

Arranging support beforehand is pertinent in better equipping you to handle retirement feelings. A possible option is researching which professional support resources are available for you to take advantage of post-retirement. Your community may even have a local support group for retired or soon-to-be-retiring individuals who regularly meet to talk and enjoy one another's company. Other soon-to-be retirees find support in talking with their already-retired friends and family members beforehand, making plans to meet up after their retirement date, and simply discussing the changes with their spouse to ready them for the transition.

Stage Two: Anticipation

As your retirement date approaches, you'll probably feel thrilling anticipation swirling with emotions of apprehension. Being handed the reins to your freedom, similar to receiving your driver's license in the years of your youth, is exciting! However, figuring out who you are and what you will do with your newly acquired free time can be daunting, especially if you have allowed your job to define you.

Stage Three: Retirement Bliss

Also known as the honeymoon phase, this is the period when you are delighted with the casting off of your occupational identity. No deadlines, no projects, no waking up early in the mornings, no more rat race or getting stuck in traffic or worrying about being late to work! It can last for a few days, months, or years.

Unfortunately, all honeymoon phases come to an end; over time, you may lose interest in the small things that once held your interest. Things that were once special become less so when you can indulge in them whenever you want. It's like being allowed to eat your birthday cake daily; eventually, it becomes just another sweet treat.

Stage Four: Discontentment

Life is becoming familiar and routine, and not in a good way. While you may have relished being able to sleep in, catch the afternoon news, or read a book late into the evening, now you're starting to feel as if you're losing your purpose in life. It's time to dig a little deeper into who you are and what you're passionate about. Now is your opportunity to pursue worthwhile activities that hold value for you.

Stage Five: Reconditioning and Stability

After you've put in the work to discover your passions, potential, limitations, and ultimately your new identity, you will begin to see the bigger picture. There is life beyond your retirement date and plenty of it. As your horizons expand, you'll realize what matters most to you, and which things you can engage in to help support the values you've developed, while nourishing a deeply fulfilled lifestyle. How to live that dream, where your soul and body are nourished daily by meaningful and enriching activities, is the entire purpose of this book!

Stage five, sign me up, please!

It sounds inviting, doesn't it? As appealing as stage five is, it is the culmination of some serious work in the form of soul-searching. It begins with shaping your identity in retirement. Peel back the layers of what you think retirement should look like, perfect or otherwise. These are made up of ideals that society has imposed upon us; depictions of elegantly gray-haired people traveling regularly and enjoying daily Tai-Chi in the park with friends. They are also formed by often negative beliefs propagated by your work environment and unhelpful influences in your life, such as those who tell you that retirement signifies "The End." Also, reframe your own idea of what you thought retirement should be, likely a culmination of both the negative and positive representations you have seen and heard.

Once you have your blank canvas on your concept of retired life, you can start painting it with the many things that will form your new multifaceted identity. What is truly remarkable about completing this process, as a fifty-five-plus-year-old individual, is that you have lived half a lifetime. You now have the experiences and knowledge and a better, more profound sense of self than when you were young, embarking on this process of self-discovery. The pressures of society, supporting a family, and making a name for yourself are arguably less. Fully explore your potential and limitations as you delve into your undiscovered self and reckon it with your discovered self. You haven't lost any part of your identity. Truth be told, you are now adding to your identity!

Ask yourself, what did you 'used to' enjoy before work? What little things piqued your interest as an adult that you previously never had time to pursue? I encourage you not to think trivially about these things but to concentrate your effort on them, laying a solid foundation for what's to come. As you ponder the aspects of your still-forming identity, it can be helpful to try and frame them within a concept known as PERMA. Positive psychologist Martin Seligman devised this acronym with five elements that are believed to contribute to a happy and fulfilling life. Here is a breakdown of PERMA.

Positive Emotion - Hope, gratitude, contentment, and feelings of positivity towards life.

Engagement - Involvement in a task or activity in which you could get lost and quickly lose track of time; you are so absorbed in it.

Relationships - Solid relationships with like-minded positive people.

Meaning - Finding a purpose greater than yourself and taking steps to support the cause.

Accomplishment - Setting goals, big or small, and taking pride in achieving them.

Searching for activities, causes, and relationships that bring you joy, create a sense of purpose for your life, and let you feel that you are achieving something will help you regain your footing in retirement. Soon your blank canvas will be a vibrant work of art, composed of all of the colors, mediums, and layers that make up you! Reinvention is daunting. No one asks for adversity at this stage in life, but it is often the push needed to make a change.

"Don't ever feel like your best days are behind you. Reinvention is the purest form of hope. Make today your best yet!"

— PHIL WOHL

Don't waste any of your coming years; embrace the emotions you're going through so you can enjoy the essentials. Aspects like developing your artistic side or getting better in tune with your intrinsic motivations. It's a moot point telling you not to let your job define you, as it no longer does. Your identity is what and who you are. Claim it!

ACTIVITY

☐ Which stage of retirement do you think you're now in? Why?

✎...

✎...

☐ What three things did you 'used to enjoy' before your working life?

✎...

✎...

✎...

☐ Which of the below emotions are most prominent for you at this point in life? And take a moment to think, Why do you feel this emotion or emotions?

- ☐ Happiness
- ☐ Anxiety
- ☐ Fear
- ☐ Disgust
- ☐ Anger
- ☐ Sadness
- ☐ Uncertain
- ☐ Surprised
- ☐ Excitement

2

ACTIVITIES TO DEVELOP YOURSELF DURING YOUR GOLDEN YEARS

*S*elf-improvement should not stop when you retire. It's necessary for you to make yourself better at what you do — making you happier and more positive in life.

They say you should never stop learning, which is true, but arguably the same can be said for self-improvement. You should never cease trying to improve yourself! This chapter will discuss some great self-improvement ideas. These high-level ideas are a great place to start but will be broken down in future chapters, offering you more detailed activities that promote self-improvement.

What is self-improvement? It's a buzzword that seems to get tossed around a lot without any clear definition.

That's in part because self-improvement can look different for everyone. It is defined as improving one's knowledge, self, or character. Those are pretty broad areas! Improving yourself simply means bettering multiple facets of your life. It can be your physical health, mental well-being, skill set, knowledge or character. Knowing what self-improvement entails, it isn't difficult to understand why it is a necessity at any age. I shudder to think what would happen to myself and my relationships if I decided never to improve on some of those areas of my life.

Self-improvement is a worthy pursuit, so valuable you can argue that it should last a lifetime; this includes retirement. If you're not entirely sold on self-improvement, check out all the benefits of continual self-work.

Promotes Self-Awareness. It's easy to sweep your emotions under the rug when working full-time and managing duties outside of your career, like looking after the family. Sure, you may experience an occasional outburst or briefly note a passing feeling; but you don't really have time to dwell on why you feel or behave the way you do. Well, now that you have all the time in the world, self-awareness can rise to the forefront. Self-awareness is the ability to objectively consider and evaluate your feelings and behaviors and how they affect one another.

What's more, you can use these findings to bring your motives, values, and interests into more precise focus. See where I'm going with this? Self-awareness is the first step in self-improvement. You can't improve on anything if you don't know where you stand! Self-awareness helps us strengthen our own emotions, thoughts, and behaviors. It enhances our relationships, allows us more influence over outcomes, and ultimately leads to a happier state of being.

Improve Strengths. Were you once able to influence a boardroom? Hold the attention of a classroom of five-year-olds? Defuse a tense customer situation? Send a convincing email to a difficult client? Were you able to patiently listen to a colleague facing a tough time and give them some solace? Have you put a smile on someone's face by an act of kindness. Did you cheer up a sad person by cooking them a warm meal? All of these abilities shed light on your strengths. Just because you are retired doesn't mean you lost any of these talents or won't have to use them again. Knowing your strengths and building upon them can help you set attainable goals and achieve them. If you remember, achievement is one of the secrets to a good life.

Conquer Weaknesses. You can't have strengths without weaknesses. We all have them, but we don't all come to terms with them. Acknowledging your weaknesses as a part of your identity lets you better understand the challenges you may face and what needs to be done to prepare for those challenges. When we recognize our shortcomings and work to identify their root cause, we can begin turning those weaknesses into strengths!

Embrace New Experiences. For too long, you have been living in your comfort zone! Self-improvement is an opportunity to break free from the routine and try something new, as is often required to learn new skills and build character. Comfort is often the opposite of growth, as being comfortable can equate to stagnancy. Retirement is the ideal time to live a little more.

Supports Mental Health. Focusing on self-evolution can be a big boon to your mental health. Those who aren't self-aware can have less control over their reactions and emotions, which usually means more stress, anxiety, and moodiness. When you devote time to improving your knowledge or yourself, you are making an effort to better your mental health and emotional well-being.

Bolsters Relationships. Self-work naturally leads to improved relationships with others. Better command of your feelings, actions, and reactions leads to happier relationships with family and friends. You can listen empathetically and build stronger bonds.

Cultivates a Sense of Purpose. Improving yourself is incredibly motivating. With each gain you make in understanding yourself on a deeper level, overcoming weaknesses, and strengthening your positive traits, your desire to continue your journey increases. Evolving and the motivation to do so eventually become a continual cycle of purpose-filled development.

Encourages a Learning Attitude. It is never too late to learn something new. Retirement poses the perfect opportunity to try and explore new things. Jump-start your retirement with a deep dive into self-improvement, and set the tone for the years to come. Working towards getting to know yourself on a deeper level instills a learning attitude that overflows into multiple areas of your life.

Promotes Self Love. Self-improvement doesn't mean making changes to yourself because you're unhappy with who you are. Instead, it means bettering yourself because you love and care about yourself. Improve yourself because you want to have a deeper understanding of your identity and live a more fulfilled and meaningful life that aligns with that identity.

A Source of Entertainment. I don't mean that self-improvement allows you to laugh at yourself, though sometimes it does. Instead, self-improvement is a task or activity that can bring entertainment to your days by offering you something concrete to focus on. It is an enriching, uplifting, motivating, and worthy cause.

"I am still learning."

— MICHELANGELO, AGE 87

DEVELOPING YOURSELF BY LEARNING NEW THINGS

Improving yourself is a form of learning, and learning new skills can be considered self-improvement. However, mastering a new skill has benefits and joys all of its own. Retirement is prime time to take up a new challenge. It can be trying something entirely new or reacquainting yourself with an old favorite that you hadn't been able to devote time to while working.

Whatever you want to learn, know that it will serve you well in retirement. Studies have found that the act of learning may help some individuals avoid or delay the onset of Alzheimer's and Dementia. More years of education is linked to a delayed start of memory problems. Like learning a new language, cognitive building activities might even help improve your brain's health, staving off memory issues that can plague seniors. Interacting with others can also help maintain neural pathways. Engaging with friends or family in significant ways might even do more for your cognitive function than completing a puzzle or a crossword.

Learning new skills can improve the quality of your life as a senior because doing so can help you preserve a healthy mind. Being physically fit allows you to enjoy the other things in life. Suppose you choose to pursue a skill that requires you to be physically and mentally active. In this case, you'll be accomplishing two critical tasks. Physical activity is vital at any age, but seniors, in particular, can reap health benefits from moving every day. It isn't a secret that parts begin to wear out as we age, and ailments can arise. However, most things can be fended off with a positive mindset and a bit of physical activity. No matter the intensity or duration, staying active after retirement is paramount. If you want to focus on your overall health, aim to enjoy activities that provide both physical and cognitive stimulation daily.

Unfortunately, for some women, retirement can coincide with menopause. This milestone can bring about increased challenges to our well-being. It's important not to let the side effects of menopause, like sadness and weight fluctuations, get the better of us! Keeping active both mentally and physically will help counteract negative menopausal symptoms. Additionally, engaging with your community and socializing might help you find your tribe. Other women who are going through the same thing as you and on whom you can lean for support.

Aside from your physical and mental well-being, a new skill can become a source of extra income! For some, it may seem a little early to be jumping back into the business talk. Nevertheless, financial well-being is a constant stressor for many retired seniors. Even if you planned well, it never hurts to have an additional source of income. Your pursuit of a new skill can often evolve into a hobby and eventually a side job. Whether crafting items, tutoring kids, trading stocks, or even writing a column, there are many activities that you might consider a pleasant pastime. You'll be pleasantly surprised to learn that others will delightedly pay you for it!

One of my colleagues retired in her late seventies. I can describe her two most vital personality traits as passionate and stubborn, and they often went hand in hand. She walked a half-mile to work and back home every day, no matter the conditions. When we met for lunch a few months after her retirement, she was still walking almost everywhere. When she did take the bus, it was to attend a self-defense class she had enrolled in, attend her weekly cardio drumming group, make it to a friend's house for book club, or go with her church community for a charity event. I was bowled over by how active she continued to be, both mentally and physically. I wondered, didn't she want to relax? After all, she had certainly earned it! Instead, she told me that what she had achieved was her freedom. Freedom to be who she wanted to be. To try new things, develop herself personally, and enjoy the challenge of taking charge of her identity. Sure, some days, she slept in or lounged in the sun reading a book, but she saw potential, not placidity when she retired.

Never have I heard my friend utter any form of negative self-talk. She has not once said, "I've never been good at..." I believe it is because she embraces retirement with an open mind and takes the leap to continually try new things, even if she didn't enjoy them as a kid, a young adult, or in middle age. Your passions may likely have changed; don't impose barriers on yourself by holding on to your old identity. Be present and proactive, open to trying new things and seizing opportunities like never before. There are many ways to develop yourself mentally, physically, and personally.

Let us now go over some ideas and concepts at a very high level to start with, as we will go deeper into some of these topics in later chapters.

1. Meditation and Mindfulness. Meditation and mindfulness go hand in hand. When you set aside time to train your brain to focus on a specific thing or simply to be present, you often achieve a state of clarity and calmness. Try a meditation routine daily for twenty-one days, and you'll be pleasantly surprised at the difference this will make in your well-being. You could start by searching for some vlogs on meditation on YouTube and pick whichever you like in terms of time and content. Or you could find your own personal meditation instructor online or in-person and take it from there. You could even write your own meditation script and get it recorded to listen to during your meditation sessions.

2. Diversify Your Diet. Eating healthier is an excellent way to improve your physical and mental state. Trying unique ingredients, learning new recipes, and taking a cooking class can make eating better more fun and exciting.

3. Chase Your Passion. Or passions! Is there something you have always wanted to do? Maybe write a book, run a marathon, or start a community project? Now's the time to pursue it wholeheartedly.

4 Get Up Early. Hear me out; getting up a half-hour earlier than you did for work could stave off health issues. Getting too much sleep in retirement could prevent you from using your brain and body as much as is needed to stay fit, physically and cognitively. While sleeping in and getting up late may be enjoyed for a short while post-retirement, it's best not to make a habit of it.

5. Slow Down Your Mornings. This is the dream of all your still-working counterparts; to be able to wake up, enjoy their coffee or tea, and gradually embrace the world around them. Open a window, listen to the birds, watch the light fall across the landscape and take notice of the world waking up! It is magical!

6. Begin a Gratitude Journal. A gratitude journal is a perfect way to maintain motivation and renew your sense of purpose. When you write down what you're thankful for, you're focusing on the positive things in your life and reflecting on how you can continue to engage with them. Plus, a gratitude journal may lower stress and improve your heart health! Start by buying your dedicated journal or notebook. Each morning after waking up, close your eyes and bring to mind three things you feel grateful for that morning, pen them down in your journal, and add the date.

7. Meaningfully Engage with Someone Else. Did you know that making a difference in someone's life can be as simple as smiling? You can also use your strengths to impact others positively. For example, offering after-school tutoring or volunteering with a local community service team. We will explore this in detail in the coming chapters.

8. Gift Yourself a Pampering Treatment. Self-care isn't selfish. Indulging in a monthly massage or spa visit can have various mental and physical health benefits. It's rejuvenating and relaxing.

9. Try Learning a New Language. Learning a new language has so many benefits, such as improved memory, better problem solving, and more flexible thinking. Which language was you most fascinated by as a child or teen? Did you ever wish you knew how to speak or read that language? Well, now is the time to learn it. Get yourself an audio course or sign up for a class to learn that language.

10. Random Acts of Kindness. Did you know that helping others can help your mental health? What's more, it will improve others' well-being, making the world a happier place! It can be as easy as handing out free water bottles in a park on a hot sunny day or paying for another person's coffee order in line behind you. There are hundreds of opportunities each day to show someone else kindness, and you'll see them when you start to look around.

11. Learn Self-Defense. For a woman, knowing self-defense is a valuable life skill. Martial arts classes often incorporate self-defense moves that are great for your body and mind, irrespective of your age. Search your local community for self-defense training programs. You can even consider Karate or Kenpo!

12. Go Back to School. Returning to school is the epitome of learning new things. Community colleges, universities, and local classes have welcomed older learners with open arms. You should never feel like you are too old to go back to school; it could be the start of a new beginning.

13. Watch a Sunset. Think of all the sunsets you missed working late or commuting home. Take some time to enjoy the sun slipping from view; you'll often feel an increased sense of gratitude for the world around you and be amazed at the beautiful colors in nature.

14. Embrace the Outdoors. Getting back to nature can lower your stress, increase your energy levels, boost your mood, and provide you with some much-needed vitamin D. Spending time outside is usually something working individuals can't do very often, so take advantage of this opportunity to get back to the basics. Start by taking a ten-minute walk any time of the day—maybe soon after you wake up or after a light lunch, or before your evening tea. Enjoy the fresh air and nature.

15. Conquer Your Fear or Work On Your Weaknesses. Remember that thing you have always put off because of too little time? Now that you have all the time in the world use it to build a better you by overcoming your fears. Not a fan of heights? Try accepting that invitation to a rooftop dinner. Learn to swim and get over your fear of the water. Of course, we recommend you do all of this with a trusted friend or family member or alongside a professional and in baby steps. But there is no time like the present to start tackling whatever makes you trepidatious!

16. Expand your Cultural Knowledge. Learning another language is fantastic, but it doesn't have to stop there! Broaden your understanding of other religions and cultures by doing your own research, attending events, going to museums or cultural hubs, and even taking a class or two. It will help deepen your appreciation for others, recognize different perspectives, and overcome biases.

17. Start a Skincare Routine. It's never too late to start a skincare routine; you will always notice the benefits despite age. When you look good, you feel good! Taking care of your skin will likely boost your confidence and self-esteem. Plus, a daily self-care routine can help you feel happy and fulfilled. Depending on your preferences, skin tone, skin type, and facial features, it's good to identify which beauty brands you prefer or trust, for all or some of these skincare products —cleanser, toner, moisturizer, primer, concealer, foundation, lip colors, eyes and eyebrow shade pencils or liners, face wash, body cleansers, lotions, creams, face pack, scrubs or masks. Maintaining your personal list of trusted products and brands is always handy.

18. Care for Your Hair. In the same vein as skincare, visiting the salon once every four to six weeks is like a special self-care treat you can look forward to. It will help you to interact with others while allowing you to relax and pamper yourself a bit. You may not have to worry about a bad hair day at work, but well-kept hair can often make your mood great. Think about it!

19. Get a Manicure or Pedicure. I was always envious of the women who had time, or should I say made time, to get their nails done. In retirement, we can all be one of those ladies! Taking time for yourself will help you look and feel great, but it can also have health effects. Lower stress and blood pressure, improved mood, and decreased muscle tension can all be fruits of "me time." If a spa trip or a professional appointment isn't in the budget, that's okay! Relaxing at home or doing your own manicure while watching your favorite TV show can still positively affect your well-being while not negatively affecting your bank account.

20. Go for That New Hairstyle. I remember my mother always pointing out a specific hairstyle that she wanted whenever she would see it on television or in magazines. I'm not sure what was holding her back, but I hope she will go for it now that she is retired! You no longer have to fit someone else's idea of what a businesswoman or a teacher should look like. Take the leap and lop off those locks!

21. Create Your Own Mantras. Mantras are statements that are repeated frequently, alone or in silence. Often, they are positive in nature and help to affirm a feeling or mindset. Create a few mantras that will help you. Your own Mantras that will boost your confidence, increase your sense of self-worth and calm, and motivate you in some way. Write them down, stick them on places you look at frequently around your room, and practice saying them to yourself throughout the day. Here are a few of my own Mantras:

I align with peace, good health, harmony, and abundance.
I am at peace with who I am and where I am in life.
All is well.

I am loveable and valuable.

I am beautiful inside out.

I love my life, and I'm grateful for this precious life.

I am in charge of how I feel, and today I choose happiness.

I choose positive, uplifting, and happy thoughts.

I am kind, I am peaceful, I am happy and I am enough.

I am worthy of all the good things in life.

22. Give Back to Your Community. There are so many reasons to volunteer during retirement. It can help replace the lack of social companionship you may feel; it's a great way to keep your brain active, and it often encourages physical activity and connects you with others outside of your generation. However, perhaps the most crucial benefit is the good you're doing for others, enriching their lives and showing them kindness. We'll delve into this in detail in chapter 11. In the meantime, a few ways you can volunteer are reading stories at your local library, joining a community program, helping other seniors, sponsoring a few food items for a local charity event, serving on a committee, or even by micro-volunteering, such as signing a petition for a good cause.

23. Consider Consulting. You have a wealth of experience and knowledge that those around you could greatly benefit from. As a bonus, sharing your advice through consulting could earn you extra money! Consulting for fun can be done on your schedule, working when you want to, and setting your own deadlines!

24. Expand Your Circle of Friends. Loneliness is a familiar feeling amongst newly retired seniors. Your coworkers may have composed a significant part of your circle of friends. There are a lot of others in the same phase as you; connecting with them through community-organized outings, interest groups, and classes is a great way to build back up your friend base.

25. Keep in Step with Technology. Learning new technology skills because you *want* to and not because you have to can be a game-changer. You might be surprised how much you enjoy picking up new tricks! Plus, it will likely enable you to communicate better with your friends and family who don't live nearby.

26. Visit Your Public Library. Your public library is a wealth of activities, events, and resources. Most have special events just for retirees and hold activities geared towards specific interests. Go to read and socialize or attend an event to meet others with whom you will have something in common!

27. Become Part of an Accountability Group. No matter what goal you are pursuing, an accountability group can help you achieve your objectives and motivate you along the way. There are plenty of forums offering virtual support, or you can search for an in-person group using social media. If you feel daring, you can even start your own accountability group.

28. Practice Forgiveness. Practicing forgiveness will bring you peace. Clearing the air will allow you to move forward and fully enjoy your life. Let go in your heart and make amends if necessary. You might just renew relationships that will bring you joy and satisfaction during your retired years.

It's never too late to engage in these activities. Learning and taking care of yourself are both lifetime pursuits. Trying new things will benefit you mentally and physically and boost social relationships. You can pursue your hobbies informally or go back to school to work towards your dream career. It is "your" time; use it in a way that leaves you feeling profoundly fulfilled and genuinely enriched.

"Anyone who stops learning is old, whether at twenty or eighty. Anyone who keeps learning stays young."

— HENRY FORD

Learning something new, improving yourself, and mastering old skills takes a bit of effort. But it is important to reframe your idea of work now that you're retired. You no longer have to feel pressure doing these things because you're not doing it as a job, and most importantly, you're not doing it for someone else. You are pursuing your passions, working on your character, and boosting your health. The pursuit of knowledge, abilities, and enlightenment in retirement is for pleasure and entertainment. Preserve the purity of simply enjoying it! Once you retrain your brain to see these forms of self-work as a form of joyous enrichment, there won't be enough hours in your day to learn and experience everything you desire to.

ACTIVITIES

☐ Check out Meditation classes or online meditation videos that you can relate to.

☐ Start a Gratitude Journal. Write three things you're grateful for, every morning.

☐ Create your skincare routine and write it down here.

✐...

✐...

✐...

☐ Create your hair care routine and write it down here.

✐...

✐...

☐ Schedule your salon appointments.

✐...

✐...

☐ Which is your nearest public library? Find out the activities or clubs this library runs and plan a visit.

✐...

✐...

☐ What is one fun activity you always wanted to do but were afraid to do?

✐...

✎...

☐ What special skills can you use to help or mentor others?

✎...

✎...

✎...

☐ Write down your own top three special feel-good Mantras that will be your guiding light for the coming years.

✎...

✎...

✎...

☐ Write these Mantras on a paper or card and stick it on the mirror you look at first thing in the morning.

WEEKLY PLANNER

☐ Create your daily schedule and routine and write it down on this page.

	Sunday	Monday	Tuesday	Wednesday	Thursday	Friday	Saturday
5am - 6am							
6am - 7am							
7am - 8am							
8am - 9am							
9am - 10am							
10am - 11am							
11am - 12pm							
12pm - 1pm							
1pm - 2pm							
2pm - 3pm							
3pm - 4pm							
4pm - 5pm							
5pm - 6pm							
6pm - 7pm							
7pm - 8pm							
8pm - 9pm							
9pm - 10pm							
10pm - 11pm							
11pm - 12am							
12am - 5am							
Notes							

3

NURTURING YOUR RELATIONSHIPS AND DEEPENING BONDS

*R*etirement can bring many positive aspects to your relationship, whether you are married or not. Permanent separation from work means that you will have lots more time to spend with your partner. Pre-retirement, it isn't uncommon for couples to look forward to all of the one-on-one time soon to come their way. Similarly, single individuals might utilize their time more on their relationships and dating life. It's a beautiful opportunity to meet new people and mingle with those in the same stage of life as you. If dating has always taken a back seat to work, then retirement might be a prime time to recommit to finding someone special. Unfortunately, the other side of the coin can sneak up on us if we are not careful.

A negative relationship, especially with your partner, can ruin retirement. Conversely, retirement can destroy a relationship.

That is quite an impactful statement, isn't it? How can you achieve happiness both in your relationships and in your retirement? Or, have your cake and eat it too, if you will.

This chapter won't focus solely on romantic relations between spouses or partners; nevertheless, it's crucial to devote some time to this significant type of relationship. Mainly, because a healthy and happy relationship with your spouse or partner can substantially impact how satisfied you are with your retirement. What's more, your marriage can be significantly affected by retirement.

However, all types of relationships can play a role in how satisfied you feel in retirement. If there is discord between you and your family or friends, life can be stressful. On the other hand, if all of your relationships are solid and fulfilling, continuing to nurture them can make your life much more joyful and purpose-filled.

"Anything is possible when you have the right people to support you."

— MISTY COPELAND

RETIREMENT AND YOUR ROMANTIC RELATIONSHIP

Earlier in this book, I mentioned how important it is to plan your emotional support before retiring. One of the suggestions I gave on doing this was to discuss how retirement can change your relationship with your partner or spouse.

We would like to believe that retirement would change our relationship for the better. We have more free time to spend with our spouse, nurturing the connection and reigniting the passion that we never had time for while working. But therein lies the problem. During the busiest years of our lives, while working and raising a family, the relationship with our partner can often be put on the back burner. It is easy to focus on life's many demands and overlook the tiny fractures in our relationships. However, the cracks become glaringly obvious when everything else is removed from the picture. Sometimes, there is no denying that you have neglected your marriage and that you no longer know who you are or who you both are as a couple.

The adjustment typically isn't easy for anyone involved. Both of you now need to re-establish your sense of self-worth and figure out how to make the other person feel valued and respected. Though you may have been sharing a home for the past few decades, chances are your identities and most of your existences were very separate from one another. Now, each of you may struggle to relearn yourself as well as your partner. You'll need to work together to become a united front during the transition.

Conversation is of prime importance here.

Talking openly about your needs, emotions and shifting roles can go a long way in lessening feelings of loneliness, rejection, and confusion. You may each have differing opinions about how much time you should spend together, how to make one another feel respected and loved, and what your new roles will look like at home. It's entirely possible that you want to shed your homemaker image and have your husband focus on cooking dinners for a change. Perhaps your partner is excited to spend more time with you, but having them constantly around makes you feel smothered. Negotiating and discussing all of these things will save you from spending months or years feeling unhappy in retirement. Evaluating your roles, wishes, and goals is essential before making a good plan for spending a happy retirement.

Maintain open lines of communication, toss out habits that no longer serve your changing needs, and remember why you loved each other in the first place. You finally have the time to renew your relationship, participate in joint activities, and fully invest in one another. Don't waste precious years of your retirement awkwardly navigating your shifting relationship; embrace the transition and find relationship satisfaction in retirement.

NURTURING ALL RELATIONSHIPS

Now that you have more time for yourself and those who matter to you, make the best of it by nurturing your relationships with your family and friends. You'll have people you talk with regularly and others you haven't spoken to in years. The good news is that it's never too late to pick up the threads and mend your relationships. Retirement can be a surprisingly lonely time unless you make an effort to connect with others. Our family is often life's most significant safety net. They can support us emotionally, financially, and even physically! You've spent a lot of time working on your profession; your relationships deserve that same, or even more, devotion and effort.

Start with your immediate family: your spouse and your children. Then, expand outwards to your parents, siblings, cousins, and distant relatives. Family membership is irrevocable. It has a rich influence on our lives, both positive and negative.

Similarly, your retirement affects you and everyone else in your inner circle. Everyone, in some form, has to realign. While doing so, the support you can offer one another is instrumental in strengthening your familial ties.

Younger retirees have an opportunity to help the next generation in so many ways, from passing down knowledge and experience to even supporting them physically or financially, such as caring for grandchildren or sponsoring childcare expenses. Grandparenting is often one of the most fulfilling retirement activities. Same-generation relations, like siblings, can be a wealth of support and entertainment. What's terrific about pursuing all of these relationships is while they'll certainly benefit you, doing so can feel like one of the least self-indulgent parts of retirement. You are meaningfully and productively investing your time in others.

Don't forget to cultivate relationships with those who feel like family—your friends and neighbors. Reconnect, rebuild, and strengthen bonds to create a source of satisfaction, enrichment, and joy in your retirement. Retirement can be considered a sacred time for friendship - meaning your wealth of experience and knowledge, coupled with more significant amounts of free time, enables you to be more selective about who you spend time with. You can choose to rebuild your community with those who will positively influence your life.

A few of your colleagues may have actually been great friends. If you're thinking of retiring soon, here's what one retiree advises you to do now: "Make an effort to maintain that friendship after you no longer see each other at work. Pinpoint your true friends and make a plan to stay in touch." For a great number of us, our work colleagues provide excellent socialization. Still, they may not turn out to be lifelong friendships. I once heard a piece of wise thought: "If your coworker relationships are based on commiseration, they won't survive retirement."

It can be valuable for those who aren't yet retired to build relationships with individuals outside of work. Hence, you have a community independent of your peers. If you are already retired, step outside of your comfort zone. Take up something you didn't do before retirement so you can meet new people with a common interest. Even if you don't meet your new best friend, socialization helps fill the void left by your work environment.

I think of my friend John's story. He was a social person, both in and out of work. As the warehouse manager, he interacted with plenty of people. And outside of work, he had a lot of friends. He bowled, played pool, and golfed. Some of his circle were those he worked with, some were childhood friends from school, and a few were teammates with a common interest. John's entire lifestyle was social, which served him well in retirement. Even though he worked at the same company for forty-seven years, his coworkers became acquaintances once he retired. The work relationships dissolved while his after-hours relationships held firm. His social life outside of work had always been separate, distinct, and healthy. In retirement, those friendships held firm, supporting him and continuing to enrich his life.

Unfortunately, not all of us will have the same story as John. Suppose your friendships outside of work took a backseat to your career colleagues. In that case, it will take energy, courage, and optimism to regenerate that circle of friends, but it is a worthy venture.

"There is only one thing more precious than our time, and that's who we spend it on."

— LEO CHRISTOPHER

Let us now look at some lovely ideas on nurturing your relationships post-retirement:

29. Renew Your Vows. Reminiscing when you first fell in love is a powerful tool to reconnect with your spouse. What better way to remember the past than renewing your wedding vows? It provides an excellent opportunity to bring family and friends together and refresh those relationships that might have been put on the back burner. Why not go to the same venue where you first made the vows to make it even more special?

30. Plan a Surprise Party. For you, your partner, a family member, or a friend! Organizing a surprise party will involve you reaching out to others and working as a group to make sure the event goes off without a hitch. Not only will this have you socializing, but it will also instill a wonderful sense of purpose!

31. Second Honeymoon. Spark the romance with a visit to your honeymoon destination. Reconnecting is vital for retired couples who have just emerged from a period of emotional distance and self-focus. A trip back to where it all began could be just the remedy!

32. Experience Nature Together. There are many ways to get into nature with your spouse or partner. Doing so can improve your happiness, health, and creativity. Additionally, nature is believed to promote healing and improve your overall well-being. It's the perfect setting to strengthen your bond and repair any past issues. Spend time talking to each other in your garden or just go for a daily stroll in the park together.

33. Scrapbook Your Love Story. Your love story has a beginning, but there is no end. Make a scrapbook filled with your cherished memories, photos, and mementos. Each year on your anniversary, you can add to it, creating a piece of family memorabilia for your kids and grandkids to enjoy.

34. Get Active Together. Healthy communication and a healthy body—joining a fitness class or participating in physical activity with your partner accomplish both! It's also an ideal way to practice togetherness without feeling overwhelmed. Why not start by looking around for fitness classes or fun sports events that couples can sign up for?

35. Care For Your Grandchildren. There are so many positives to babysitting your grandchildren, grandnieces, nephews, or any relation of a younger generation! By doing so, you're helping others in a variety of ways. It may be physically, financially, or emotionally. You're also enriching the next generation with your wealth of knowledge and experiences. In turn, they provide you with a bit of physical activity and likely entertainment, too.

36. Arrange a Romantic Date. Sometimes, it can be hard to connect with your partner; free time suddenly feels like a magnifying glass in your relationship. Reignite the passion by organizing a romantic date for the two of you. Planning will be fun to occupy your time, but the lasting relationship effects of the date can be much more profound. Why not start by finding a good restaurant in your locality and making a dinner booking for just the two of you?

37. Plan for The Future. If you haven't already, consider creating a will. You may be surprised just how fun a traditionally grim task can be. It's lovely planning for the future and ensuring your loved ones and your possessions are taken care of. The detail-oriented job is also a tremendous challenge for your brain, keeping your neural pathways open and active.

38. Connect with Childhood Friends. Reconnecting with long-lost friends has never been easier, thanks to the internet and social media. Chances are, they're in a similar life stage as you and just waiting to grow friendships. Reach out to them and just say "Hi"!

39. Host a Movie Night. These days everyone loves watching movies on online platforms. Imagine how fun it will be to host a movie night at your home to watch a newly released movie. Invite your close girlfriends and watch the movie together, enjoying popcorn and hot chocolate.

40. Go on a Blind Date. There is no time like the present! If you are single and want to explore new relationships, meeting new people can be nerve-wracking, especially when it's more than a casual friendship. However, stepping out of your comfort zone to make new acquaintances offers socialization while strengthening multiple self-improvement areas.

41. Make and Decorate Baked Goods with Kids. It can be your family members or get involved with a community event. Libraries and community centers often have cooking classes or demonstrations that might need volunteers. Baking and decorating is a fantastic outlet for your creativity.

42. Organize a Friendly Snowball Fight. No, age is not a criterion here! Organizing a snowball fight with your friends will give you all a healthy reason to get outdoors and get involved with one another. If you don't have snow, pick up some soft cloth toy balls!

43. Catch Up with Old Colleagues. Not all coworkers are simply coworkers. If you have a few peers who became best pals, regularly meeting with them for a meal is an excellent way to catch up, stay connected, and have something on your calendar to look forward to.

44. Make a Family Photo Album or Tree. Assembling all of your family's history is often exciting and fun. Still, I would be lying if I said it isn't time-consuming. Tracing your lineage and compiling photos and documents is often one task that is put off because you never have enough time. Now that you do, invest in this valuable task that can be enjoyed for generations to come. Start by organizing your photos and memories in order of date. Why not create a photo album or photo book for life's different phases and chapters?

45. Visit Long-Lost Relatives or Friends. Can you think of a lovelier excuse to travel? No longer do you need to put off going to see those relatives who were always too far away to visit; make a fun trip out of it!

46. Thank You's All-Around. Purchase a pack of thank you cards in bulk, 50–100. Then, every day, take a moment to write a card or two to all friends, family, colleagues, and acquaintances who you have come across in your life. It is simply a note to say "Thank you" for their part in your life, no matter how small, and to let them know you remember them.

47. Road Trip with Your Best Friend. Many retirees love to travel; it helps expand their physical and mental horizons. Traveling with your best friend can help you feel more comfortable with being adventurous. The skills and communication required for a road trip will improve your brain health and keep you sharp. Your journey can be short or long, frugal or splurge-worthy; you're in the driver's seat!

48. Mentor Others. Mentorship is an honor that you've earned. Your life well-lived has served you with the experience and knowledge to guide others. You can impart your expertise to the next generation if you possess a skill. Mentoring will boost your socialization, strengthen your knowledge, and increase your connections network. It can be anything from teaching a little kid how to bake a cookie to grooming a young lady for her first job interview. Anything you can do to help someone with your knowledge and life experience will be so valuable.

49. Make a Baked Goodie for Someone Special. Cooking and baking are enjoyable pastimes; doing it for someone else is an expression of love. It can be a small chocolate cake, freshly baked bread, a bunch of cookies, or anything you like to make. Making something for another person allows you to express your feelings and creativity; it also requires mindfulness and your full attention. Though, most of all, it is a lovely form of altruism and brings a smile to the receiver. Why not write a special note to them too!

50. Organize a Picnic in Your Local Park Or Garden. Put your planning skills to the test and organize a friendly outing filled with good food and good friends. It will challenge your thinking, encourage you to connect with other people, and present everyone with a pleasant chance to get outdoors and interact. Even better if your group of friends can take turns to arrange the picnic once in a while!

51. Socialize with Neighbors. Though those living near you may be of a different age or background, you all have one thing in common—your neighborhood! Bolster your sense of community by interacting with the people living close by. Walk around when the weather is nice, stop to chat, or drop off a treat. You'll likely find a great source of support closer to home than you once thought.

52. Visit the Setting of Your Favorite Movie. In the past, you may have traveled to destinations based on work or family preferences; now is your chance to go somewhere for yourself! How unique and special would it be to travel to the location of your favorite film? It could also be the location of a movie scene that has influenced you. A trip like this will be a joy to plan and participate in.

53. Organize a Coffee Morning. Get together with your girlfriends and have a nice chat over coffee or tea and cake! Prepare a refreshments bar so that everyone can make their own drink when they come over. Then, you can all relax and enjoy great conversations with one another.

54. Attend Your High School Reunion. Maybe you have always attended, or this is possibly your first time; either way, this is a fantastic post-retirement event. It is an opportunity to see old friends and reconnect, as well as something to look forward to.

55. Plan a Potluck Party. Potluck parties are fun and a low-key way to meet with neighbors, friends, family, or even your book club. Everyone brings a dish to share. You'll enjoy exploring new foods, enjoying old favorites, and having an opportunity to get in the kitchen yourself.

56. Call on Old Relationships. Calling a family member you haven't spoken to in a while is a brave thing to do. Overcoming this fear benefits all involved.

You will re-establish a relationship and hopefully brighten the other person's day. You never know, maybe that person was also looking forward to a call from you!

57. Make a Time Capsule for Your Family. A time capsule is a collection of items sealed into a container and locked away until a chosen date. You can include letters, photographs, sentimental items, or anything small enough to fit. The time capsule can then be buried in your back garden or stored somewhere safe. Leave your family with instructions as to when they can open it!

What is lovely about all of these activities is their versatility. Some of these ideas may sound expensive, but it doesn't have to be so. You can make them as budget-friendly or as splurge-worthy as you like. Each person's preferences and retirement plan are different. Don't discard an idea because you believe it will cost too much.

Many of these events can be simple celebrations. Renewing your vows can be a grand affair, or you can host a backyard ceremony. The activities are flexible, too. Road trip a short distance and camp, if setting off across the country seems too ambitious. It is your retirement to do with as you see fit, as long as you remember to share the journey with others!

Relationships are essential during your retirement years. You could argue building social wealth is just as important as financial wealth when it comes to achieving satisfaction in retirement. A support system can help you overcome new challenges as you age. Your friends and family are a shoulder to lean on, an ear to listen, belly laughs when you're down, and the hands cheering you on. An embracing community can help make your life in retirement rich and fulfilling.

Numerous studies proved that people who have happy and gratifying relationships with their family, friends, and local community are happier, have fewer health concerns, and live a long, satisfying life. On the contrary, a substantial lack of fulfilling social interactions is associated with depression, cognitive decline, and early mortality.

"If we don't make time for friends, we won't have any."

— THE CHOSEN

Through the activities provided above, you'll get the chance to bond with others, both familiar and new.

Talk to them about all aspects of life and have deeper conversations to form more meaningful connections.

In the next chapter, you will learn activities for discovering and nurturing your creativity. This will improve your well-being and ultimately enhance how supportive you are to those around you.

ACTIVITIES

☐ When and where did you first meet your partner?

✎...

☐ Where did you go on your honeymoon? Would you like to visit there again?

✎...

☐ Plan a surprise party for your family or friends.

☐ Plan a garden picnic for your family or friends.

☐ Name three of your childhood friends. Are you in touch with them?

✎...

✎...

✎...

□ Name three of your good colleagues and plan to catch up with them.

✎...

✎...

✎...

□ Make a family & friends photo album with all your favorite photos and memories.

□ Who is your oldest relative? Where do they live? Would you like to meet them?

✎...

✎...

4

KEEPING YOUR CREATIVE JUICES FLOWING

*W*hen was the last time you tapped into your creative side? We often have to problem solve and get creative with our thinking at work, but when did you last get creative and produce something artistic?

According to the dictionary, creativity is defined as "The use of the imagination or original ideas, especially in producing an artistic work." Another description of creativity is "A phenomenon whereby something new and valuable is formed. The created item may be intangible or a physical object." Both of these definitions share a similar idea—*creating something new.*

On your retirement journey, you're making something unique—yourself!

Every day is an opportunity to add a little more to your canvas, filling in the blanks with new colors and patterns in the form of passions and skills. Creativity will help you craft your identity throughout retirement while improving your health, mental well-being, and cognitive agility.

"Creativity is nothing but a mindset free."

— TORRIE T. ASAI

There is much fascinating research on how creativity positively affects our health.

One study found that being creative fulfilled two essential needs to feel content—the need to be challenged and the need to be stimulated. Actively participating in innovative experiences both challenges and stimulates your brain. There are a variety of reasons as to why this is conducive to your well-being.

Creativity is commonly linked to the arts, but retirees can also engage in "everyday creativity," a term popularized by Ruth Richards, by approaching life with an open mind and embracing ordinary tasks in a new way. Being creative with your hands, mind, or both can help lower stress, decrease depression, increase positivity, strengthen your problem-solving skills, and boost confidence. Expanding your view to the bigger picture to creatively solve problems is excellent for your brain health.

Creative thinking strategies draw on a myriad of neural pathways and help to fend off issues like Dementia and Alzheimer's. Creativity can help improve your mental health in less literal ways, too. Often, by helping, you become an observer of your negative feelings instead of being defined by them. Many of us have heard of the benefits of meditation. Still, it isn't always easy to let our minds wander and reach the desired meditative mood, though getting into a flow-state through artistic expression can help!

Getting into a reflective mindset can happen quite effortlessly when we focus on creating art. As you work on your project, it's natural for thoughts to float through your head. Instead of dwelling on stressful ideas, you simply acknowledge them and let them pass. Meditative art can have huge advantages if practiced regularly. Sometimes even altering the information processing part of your brain leads to lower stress, improved memory, and better moods.

Bringing people together and boosting socialization is yet another way creativity benefits retirees. Community-driven creativity opportunities, like art classes and workshops, help like-minded individuals meet one another. This type of support and connection with other passionate artists can foster a wonderful sense of well-being.

Sandra had huge creativity aspirations for her retirement. She is a dear friend of mine. She had always wanted to write a book but never seemed to have enough time. With her retirement quickly approaching, Sandra couldn't wait for the opportunity to sit down in front of her computer for hours, typing up her first novel. She also loved all art forms and desired to join a photography group or take a painting class. Often, I would listen to her animatedly describe how glorious her retirement would be, filled with artistic endeavors that appealed to her creative side.

But, post-retirement, Sandra fell into a period of isolation and loneliness, mentioning that she had trouble even getting motivated to leave the house on one of our lunch dates. A few weeks later, when we met again, I learned that it was creativity that had pulled her out of her retirement blues slump! She still wasn't comfortable going out and meeting with others in a class or group. Her daughter found a virtual writer's workshop! Members met online once a month and regularly exchanged thoughts and ideas on a virtual forum. It turned out to be just the thing Sandra needed, letting her get creative within her comfort zone and, in turn, boosting her retirement satisfaction!

Most of us have tunnel vision focused entirely on our career until retirement; now, it is time to think outside the box. Allowing yourself to experiment and create will only enhance your well-being. It will develop a positive mindset within you that will be obvious to other people. Creativity, and its positive side effects, can genuinely be contagious.

"What keeps life fascinating is the constant creativity of the soul."

— DEEPAK CHOPRA

Let us now look at a few such ideas.

58. Craft a Book. Writing carries many benefits, from improved memory to lower stress. Crafting an entire story or book may not be for everyone, but it is a life-long goal of many. You could write a whole fiction novel, create a collection of short poems, write an auto-biography, write up on any non-fiction topic you like, or simply join a writer's workshop to improve your skills. Whatever writing avenue you pursue, the act of putting words on paper is excellent for your emotional, mental, and physical health.

59. Try Floral Arrangements. Flowers are big mood boosters; working with them can promote feelings of happiness and leave you with an uplifting display. It takes focus, creativity, and problem solving to craft an aesthetically appealing bunch of blooms. Buy some flowers and create a lovely floral arrangement that you can enjoy all week long. Isn't it refreshing to have a vase of well-arranged fresh flowers on your coffee table or kitchen worktop?

60. Learn to Play an Instrument. Did you dabble in music as a child? Or have you always wanted to play an instrument? Feed your brain by pursuing a musical instrument in retirement. It's a terrific creative outlet that can lower stress, increase cognitive ability, and provide enjoyment to those around you. Why not sign up for weekly lessons to learn your favorite instruments? You can find good tutors online or within your local community.

61. Learn to Paint. You don't have to be Rembrandt; painting is in the eye of the beholder. Try your hand at oil paints, watercolors, or just wax crayons. Maybe you want to attend a paint and pour class with your girlfriends. There are infinite ways to explore painting, all of them equally fun and beneficial.

62. Take a Pottery Class. Pottery is a fantastic creative outlet that lets you work with your hands to produce something functional and beautiful. As most pottery forms require special tools, you'll likely have to enroll in a class where you can meet new people and socialize. It will feel really special when you make your first teacup or tiny flower pot.

63. Take Up Dancing. Enrolling in a dance class opens the doors to various wellness benefits. Take a salsa class with your partner and engage in creativity, physical activity, and romance. Enroll in a class to mingle with like-minded people while having fun exercising your body and mind. Dancing requires cognitive and physical skills, making it a well-rounded activity for retirees.

64. Audition For a Play. Perhaps you were a high school performer, or maybe this is how you practice self-improvement and conquer fear. Whatever the reason, auditioning for a play is a fantastic idea! Should you be cast in a production, you'll reap the benefits of regularly interacting with others, engaging with your community, and keeping your memory in tip-top shape.

65. Try a DIY Craft Project. Books, magazines, and the internet are positively bursting with DIY activities. Deciding to do a project allows you to plan, create, focus, and achieve. Drown out the stress around you by tackling a fun and unique project. Ideas include anything from simple artwork to a bespoke home renovation.

66. Learn Clay Modeling. Clay work requires that you work with your hands. It is an outlet for creativity; that can let negative emotions like stress flow from your body. If you're looking for a social, hands-on way to experiment with creativity, modeling clay it is!

67. Learn Plant Grafting. Plant grafting and budding are ways to join two plants. It can be done to create a hybrid or to make a larger plant. This horticulturist skill is fascinating. Though it's challenging, you'll feel immense satisfaction once you succeed.

68. Complete One Sudoku Puzzle a Day. Like Sudoku, number puzzles can help keep your brain years younger. One study found that a puzzle a day resulted in improved cognitive function. Plus, having a challenge each day can be a motivating part of your routine and helps keep your brain active and sharp. Grab yourself a puzzle and riddles or crosswords book and commit to doing a page or a puzzle every day.

69. Review and Resell Your Unwanted Gifts Items.
With each year of your life, you've probably accumulated quite a bit of stuff. While you're working on refining and decluttering your identity, why don't you do the same for your unwanted gift items? Take a look around and find belongings or gifts that you can resell; you'll make a bit of money and give someone else a chance to enjoy a special item. Get creative with your thinking and see if you can get by with less.

70. Create a Gift Basket. Gift baskets are such fun to make and require some serious creativity. It's a fun puzzle finding items that fit a theme and make a lovely basket. You'll have a thoughtful gift to share with a friend or family member when you're done. To get you started: You can make gift baskets with baked goodies, cookies, chocolates, sweets, and other treats, or a hamper with beauty and self-care items, or a spa gift basket. It can also be a hamper of homemade candles, soaps, wax melts, or essential oils.

71. Declutter One Room at a Time. A clean and decluttered home is a terrific start to your retirement. You don't have to do it all at once, though. Try to declutter one room each day. Think outside the box with your storage solutions, sell or give away anything you no longer need, and give your space a refresh! My mom always says if you haven't used something for over two years, there's a slim chance that you will ever use it again.

72. Start a Knitting Project. Knitting or crocheting are lovely ways to work with your hands creatively. The repetition movement is excellent at getting you into a stress-relieving flow state. Having a piece to work on bit by bit will give you something to look forward to until you finish your fantastic work of art and it will fill you with a sense of accomplishment.

73. Restyle Your Wardrobe. No, I'm not talking about shopping for all new clothes. Why not give DIY fashion a try and overhaul your old clothes yourself? You can recreate your signature style using a sewing machine or fabric paints.

74. Scrapbook the Story of You. Scrapbooking can be as straightforward or as involved as you would like it to be. You could start by adding photos of you as a baby and proceed by adding a photo of every stage in your life. You can get fancy with your embellishments or focus on adding pictures or personal mementos. Scrapbooking is fabulous for socialization, too; scrapbook with your pals and then share your book with others when you're finished!

75. Consider Soap Making. Your library likely has plenty of soap-making books, or your community may offer a few classes. It's surprisingly more manageable than you may think, and you can get incredibly creative with your soap scents, colors, and designs. You can add your own blend of natural ingredients and essential oils. This hands-on process is so satisfying and can produce terrific soap bars that make perfect holiday gifts for friends and family.

76. Attempt Candle Making. Like soap making, candle making is an enjoyable task resulting in a thoughtful handmade gift. There are lots of methods when it comes to candle making and an infinite amount of designs. Some of my favorites are realism candles that look like actual treats!

77. Create Perfumed Wax Melts. Like candle making, creating perfumed wax melts can be a lovely creative hobby and a fun side business. You can throw yourself into producing sensual and beautiful wax melts that highlight your creativity. Then, give them away as gifts or make extra money by selling them at craft shows.

78. Make a Gorgeous 5D Painting. 5D diamond painting is the perfect art form for those just dipping their toes into the world of creativity. Like paint by numbers, colorful "diamonds" or rhinestones are set onto a canvas using a paint-by-numbers style system. The result is positively stunning, while it allows you to destress, zone out, and reach a meditative state. It gets more exciting as you place each stone in the right places, and the painting emerges slowly. The result is so satisfying; you have to try it at least once!

79. Make a Snowman. If you live somewhere it snows, head out with your grandkids, friends, or even by yourself to build a friendly snowman. Working with your hands, and possibly even working up a sweat, is excellent physical activity. In the end, your creation will delight the neighborhood for as long as your snowman can resist melting!

80. Make a Snow Angel. Snow angels are another fun way to make art, get into nature, and exercise your body. Making a snow angel is something you can do just for yourself. Center yourself with the earth and create a beautiful but short-lived work of art.

81. Try Mosaic Art. Making mosaics is quite tactile, asking you to use your dexterity to craft an often intricate art piece. Everything from the craft itself to sometimes the materials used is very ancient, connecting you with the past. Mosaics themselves are very hardy and will stand the test of time. It's a fantastic way to satisfy your need to create.

82. Make a Sundial. Making a sundial can be as complex or simple as you like. Professional kits sold online will result in a gorgeous, long-lasting piece you can keep in your garden for years. Or, you can make an easy version with items you likely have lying around your home.

83. Make Outdoor Chimes. Outdoor chimes offer soothing sounds and often look lovely hanging in your garden. Chimes can be made with a variety of items. You can source shells and thin, flat rocks from the beach, then hang them with a fishing line or plastic threads. Or, you can upcycle keys, beads, or old xylophone bars. The opportunities are many!

84. Create Sand Art. There are a few ways to make incredible sand art. You can try pouring sand art into a bottle, methodically pouring layer after layer of colorful sand, by focusing and steadying your hand. Or, you can make sand art on a canvas with an adhesive. Either method provides an excellent medium in which to release your creativity!

85. Distill Your Essential Oils. If you're searching for a way to involve all your senses while getting creative, try making your own essential oils at home. Using a slow cooker, you can steam distill essential oils from plants you grew and harvested. The entire process is incredibly therapeutic, beginning with gardening and culminating in enjoying a homemade aroma. If this sounds interesting, you can start by researching how to safely distill essential oils from lavender, rose, jasmine, peppermint, or lemon balm at home.

86. Create a Travel Vision Board. You've likely learned by now that the world is a vast place. There are probably plenty of places you want to visit. Making a vision board with pictures or magazine cuttings that includes both possible and dream destinations is a beautiful way to put your imagination to good use. It can help you see your travel goals, and seeing it daily will motivate you to achieve them.

87. Write Your Own Song. Songwriting is undoubtedly a talent, but that doesn't mean we can't all take a crack at it! Like other forms of writing, creating a song allows you to express your emotions creatively. It turns into a great brain exercise to keep you mentally sharp when you attempt to pair it with music.

88. Record a Song. Today, activities once reserved for celebrities, like recording a song, are often available to the public for less than you think. Much like getting in a sound booth and recording a song! If you've always wanted to record your own music, have a piece for a loved one, or are simply a music lover, consider finding a local recording studio to make your dream come true. Now is the time!

89. Make a Video. The younger generations are always making videos, and it is surprisingly simple with today's technology. Hop on the trend and create your own mini-movie. It can be a vlog where you document your life, a tutorial, your favorite recipe, or just a fun dance trend. Movie making is surprisingly exciting, and you might enjoy letting loose by singing, dancing, or talking, even if you're the only one ever to see it.

90. Learn Flamenco Dance. Dance is a wonderful form of creative expression. The steps and movements can be considered a graceful art form. Flamenco is one of the best representations of this, based on the folk music of Spain. This gorgeous dance can be a bit complex, but learning it is a great workout for your body, mind, and soul.

91. Journal. Journaling is a creative activity that anyone can do. All you need is a piece of paper, or notebook and a pen, or just your laptop's notepad. Let your thoughts and emotions flow; you don't have to share this sacred space with anyone. It's a productive way to incorporate creativity into your daily routine that can also benefit your well-being. If you haven't tried this before, it is a good idea to start writing a few sentences or a page about any topic that comes to your mind daily. You'll see that you are getting good at writing as days pass.

92. Build an Ice or Sand Sculpture. Depending on where you live, you can be creative through nature. Building sand or ice sculpture incorporates physical activity, design thinking, fun, and problem-solving. It also helps to bring a smile to all those passing by.

93. Create DIY Paper Decor. Getting creative helps to unblock past ways of thinking and old habits. How often was the paper used for note-taking, letters, or bills during your career? Now that you're retired rethink paper and craft some gorgeous paper decor. You can make fans, flowers, paper chains, and more.

94. Make Jewelry with Silver. Jewelry making is a time-honored skill that takes practice but is worth it. Jewelry making from silversmithing is a fun challenge that takes patience and attention to detail. Depending on your interest level, time, and resources, you can make jewelry at home or get involved with a group. There are free videos online or classes that you can attend to learn the skill.

95. Try Model Building. Model building can offer you a fabulous sense of achievement once the entire project is complete. You can build a miniature replica of almost anything with concentration and talent. It is rewarding, stress-relieving, and a great way to be creative without relying on being inspired first. DIY miniature replica kits for famous buildings are available in online shops or craft stores.

96. Go Antiquing. Who knew antiquing was a way to foster creativity?! Well, it is when you reimagine your antique into a stunning piece of home decor or figure out how to give it a second life. You can turn old grain sacks into throw pillows, repurpose a dresser, or arrange them into artful focal points for your home.

97. Join a Quilters Group. Creativity can foster togetherness, especially when you get together with a like-minded group of people. Quilting is one such community where creativity and social bonding genuinely shine. Because quilting is a skill that is best taught in person, pursuing this artistic avenue can be excellent for your emotional and mental health when you feel stuck in retirement.

98. Be Part of a Theater Group. Likewise, a theater group is another excellent way to make friends and share your art form with your neighbors and community. It doesn't matter if you've always been extroverted or want to work on being brave; being part of a theater production can help. You'll feel incredibly empowered by the experience and gain a great set of friends!

99. Start a Blog. Blogging is like a journal, except in a public forum. You can choose to share your heartfelt sentiments, as you would with a personal journal, or keep things more formal. Formal blogging examples are starting a recipe blog, writing tutorials, or keeping a travel log. Not only is blogging a fantastic way to enjoy creative writing, but you can also meet new people virtually and build a remarkable online community of your own.

100. Make Chalk Murals. If you have a talent for drawing with chalk, consider making murals on your sidewalk. These fun and colorful drawings can make someone's day! It can be a drawing or a beautifully written inspirational "thought for the day." Ask local libraries, restaurants, or community centers if you can beautify their space with a neat chalk drawing.

101. Create Comic Book Art. Comic book art is unlike other types of art. It's bold, punchy, and a lot of fun to make. You can make cartoon strips or write your own comic book. There are many online tools and platforms which will make the creation easier and more fun. Make a book for your grandkids, or share your creation online!

102. Learn Silk-Screen Printing. Silk-screen printing is often used to decorate T-shirts, cups, bags, etc. The cutting and crafting machine for silk screen printing has become a popular way for people to design and print things at home. You can create your own graphics or use premade graphics online, then print and stick them on your item. Add in your passion and skill and reach out to interested people with your work, and you may have found yourself a source of extra income.

103. Learn Embroidery. Embroidery is a beautiful skill. It teaches patience while working on your dexterity and hand-eye coordination. You can embroider artwork to hang on your wall, blankets, pillowcases, or clothing. A one-of-a-kind embroidered piece makes a unique gift.

104. Feng Shui Your Home. Feng Shui is an ancient practice based on the idea that you can use energy to harmonize yourself with your home. To do this, you need to rearrange furniture and art pieces within your home to create balance. If this sounds interesting, you could do some research and then try your hand at Feng Shui in your living spaces.

105. Try Beading. Beading is a simple and beautiful way to make jewelry. With easy-to-source materials from your craft store, you can make necklaces, bracelets, and earrings. The designs can be as simple or complex as you like.

106. Take Up Lapidary. Lapidary is the art of shaping stones or gems to make them into wearable pieces, commonly jewelry. Joining a lapidary society or online forum can be a fun way to learn a new skill and make friends.

107. Try Puppetry. Have you ever tried to make a puppet? There are many ways to do it, from sock puppets to foam and felt. A wooden marionette is another idea for the creative woodworker. You'll end up with a lovely piece of art you can pass on to little kids in your circle.

108. Make a Bird Feeder. A bird feeder is a fun project that benefits our feathered friends in addition to being a fun project for you. You can make a permanent bird feeder with materials like wood and metal. Or, make a temporary bird feeder out of pinecones, string, and birdseed.

109. Craft with Perler Beads. Perler beads are tiny colorful beads that are placed onto a template. Then, you iron the beads until they melt together into a piece of artwork. You can make various shapes and images of varying sizes and colors.

"You have probably heard the saying that you can't teach an old dog new tricks. Actually, another saying that is probably more accurate, but is not quite as well known is: 'The quickest way to become an old dog is to quit learning new tricks.'"

— KENNETH L. HIGBEE

Some of the above ideas often require innate talent. You may find that you possess that talent, and you may not. But you'll never know until you try. One particularly remarkable aspect of creativity is that it helps change past ways of thinking, reshaping old habits and ideas, including negative past thoughts, such as "I'm not good at art" or "I can't think outside the box." Getting in touch with your creative side is all about breaking barriers. You will be pleasantly surprised at how many artistic things you can do and how many new skills you can learn.

You now have the time to pursue creative passions free from the demands of your pre-retirement life. You don't have a deadline, a supervisor or boss waiting to criticize you, or even the pressure to finish a project if you don't want to.

There has never been a better time to test your capabilities and enjoy attempting the unknown. You won't be the only person reaping the rewards, but also your dear ones. Many others can appreciate the gift of your artistic talents, whether it be new artwork, an insightful blog, or performing on stage.

So many of these ideas go hand in hand with your physical and mental health. Often, a new pursuit can have more rewarding benefits for your overall well-being than you realize. However, the next chapter will look at how to specifically strengthen your physical self and promote mental well-being during retirement. There are many more ways to keep yourself fit than just pickleball and puzzle games; I promise you'll find something to feed your soul and nourish your body!

ACTIVITIES

☐ Identify up to five creative ideas you would like to try from the above list.

✎...

✎...

✎...

✎...

✎...

☐ Make your own flower arrangement for your coffee table.

☐ Buy Sudoku, Crossword, or a Puzzle workbook and commit to doing a page each day.

☐ Name the person (or people) who is most dear to you.

✎...

✎...

✎...

☐ What would you include in a personal homemade gift basket for this special person?

✎...

✎...

✎...

✎...

✎...

▢ What fragrance is your favorite essential oil? Would you like to try making it at home? Write down the recipe.

✎...

✎...

✎...

✎...

✎...

▢ Create your Travel Vision Board or Wish List.

▢ Which five places would you be putting on your Travel Vision Board?

✎...

✎...

✎...

✎...

✎...

5

CHALLENGING YOURSELF MENTALLY AND PHYSICALLY

*O*ur overall health is the foundation of our happiness and success throughout our lives.

No matter how exciting our travels, fun our activities, or pleasurable our friendships are, if we're not mentally and physically healthy, we'll find it hard to enjoy them.

Retirement changes many things, but the need to be aware of the state of our mind and body remains constant. In fact, you could argue that we need to pay closer attention as our bodies age and health issues start to creep upon us.

Let me explain: As amazing as it would be to visit Paris, if I didn't keep up with my physical fitness, walking the streets of France and waiting in line to enter the Louvre Museum could be considered unpleasant. It isn't hard to envision the sore back, aching knees, and struggling cardio that could result from too little exercise and movement.

Similarly, failing to keep in tune with your mental health could also put a damper on retirement activities. A movie with friends sounds dismal if my mind is racing the entire time, overwhelmed with thoughts that could have been quelled by journaling, mediation, or simply planning my time and days with more purpose.

Our body and mind have the ability to derail our retirement, but only if we let them! Some things are inevitable as we age, but we can certainly improve or exacerbate the ailments that naturally come with aging. Your recliner shouldn't become your new go-to spot during retirement. Of course, you've earned rest and relaxation. However, I warn you to indulge in moderation! Some of us could use a retirement reset, adding more physical activity and keeping a closer eye on our mental health. Others are likely overjoyed to have more time to spend on the physically and mentally stimulating activities they have enjoyed since youth! Regardless of your feelings about staying active, aging well requires these things.

Thankfully, what's good for the body is often good for the brain. Many of these ideas incorporate both physical and mental wellness. Even if they don't, there are plenty of opportunities to combine them into a well-rounded activity that supports all aspects of your well-being. Start if you aren't regularly moving your body and exercising your mind. If you are already doing this, don't stop!

"Use it or lose it."

— ANCIENT MOTHERLY ADAGE

It is probably safe to assume that most of us don't have a problem strengthening ourselves cognitively. Practicing meditation, picking up a crossword puzzle, or simply reading an inspirational book sounds much more pleasant than getting on a stationary bike or agreeing to a round of tennis. Additionally, mental fitness activities tend to be more accessible. The majority of people claim that physical activity is a hurdle when it comes to keeping up their health.

Most people tend to shy away from exercise, so I want to make a case for why adding regular movement to your retirement routine is crucial! You can forget the reasons having to do with losing weight or getting toned, though it is excellent to look and feel your best. Physical activity benefits go beyond skin deep. Exercise can increase the quality of your health, boost your happiness, and, to a good extent, prolong your retirement years!

Let's look at why retirees need physical activity in more detail:

Encouraging bonding. Physical activity has profound effects on the brain. One such outcome is that movement primes us to engage with others. We become more receptive to bonding, communication, and connection. Just like a hug opens our minds and gives us those warm feelings, exercise produces a similar result in our brain chemistry. This chemical change is why fitness groups or classes can be so positive! Walking, working out, or moving in some way with other people fosters relationships and offers an invaluable sense of belonging.

Reduces sadness and anxiety. This is no secret; numerous studies have shown how exercise reduces hostile feelings and promotes mental positivity. Chemicals in our body tied to feelings of contentment, delight, confidence, and happiness are automatically released when we engage in physical activity. Researchers have also found that certain compounds, like myokine, are produced when muscles contract but have the ability to alter our brain structure for the better—permanently. Possibly even making our bodies better equipped to handle future stress.

Maintains balance. Yes, it might assist with physical balance, but I'm referring to your emotional sense of balance. Choosing a designated time for activity can give your days a much-needed sense of routine. Though it may seem counterintuitive to schedule your days once again, too much freedom can lead to feelings of depression, boredom, and isolation. Penciling a specific time for movement each day helps you avoid two retirement pitfalls simultaneously.

Boosts confidence. Why is exercise not at the top of everyone's retirement bucket list? Well, a workout can be challenging. But think of how empowered and accomplished you'll feel when you complete that round of walking or finish that bike ride. The sense of confidence you can gain from physical activity often flows into other areas of your life, motivating you to take on additional challenges.

Improves and maintains brain health. I've talked about how meditation is great for you. However, it understandably can be difficult for some to sit down and consciously focus. Getting into a creative flow can simulate reflection, which is also true for exercise! Like biking or walking, repetitive physical movement naturally shifts us into a meditative state. We become grounded, more aware, and reflective without making a significant mental effort.

Reduces pain and risk of ailments. Of course, an undeniable reason to keep moving is to reduce your risk of common illnesses and injuries. Doctors advise exercise can lower heart disease, osteoporosis, diabetes, and other dangers if you take time to focus on your physical health. Most individuals can easily tailor their form of exercise to suit chronic conditions, preferences, and abilities.

"When health is absent - wisdom cannot reveal itself, art cannot manifest, strength cannot fight, wealth becomes useless, and intelligence cannot be applied."

— HEROPHILUS

Please consult your doctor or health professional before trying out any new physical activity, diets, or supplements. Use appropriate safety gear, and use due diligence.

Let us now explore ways to improve and maintain your physical and mental well-being.

110. Take a Dance Class. Zumba, in particular, is an excellent workout. It incorporates dance, cardio moves, and occasionally light strength training. Often taught in a group, you can look forward to laughing and learning with other dancers! Which is your nearest dance class for seniors?

111. Run a Marathon (or a mile). For some, running a marathon is a lifelong goal. Other individuals would be happy simply to complete a mile. Whatever distance you choose, running a race is a significant accomplishment. The training and focus needed to achieve your goal will slowly boost your physical health and positively affect your stress levels. Most races have a senior division called "masters," so you'll be in good company.

112. Play Mahjong. Playing this classic Chinese puzzle game is excellent for your mental health. It helps to preserve neural pathways and keep your brain active. You can play on your own or even online. However, frequently playing with friends can be more enjoyable and mentally stimulating. Search your community for a local league or group.

113. Run a Charity Race. Running is excellent for your well-being, but what if you could make all of your training even more meaningful? When you run a race for your local community's charity, all your hard work benefits not only you but also a worthy cause. In most instances, a portion of your registration fee goes to a charity with the option to raise additional funds by soliciting friends and family to support you.

114. Read a Religious Book. Challenge yourself to read the prime Holy Book according to your religion or faith, cover to cover. Build a time into your day to read the Holy Scriptures and make this time a priority. Try to read a chapter or a page per day from your Holy Book, and stick to it. The wisdom, peace, and insight you get in this process is true nourishment to your soul. I promise. Reading the Holy Bible every morning helps me stay calm, hopeful, grateful, and focused in life.

115. Do a Color Run. The goal of a color run is to be happy and healthy; this sounds like what we all want for retirement! Sign up and run a color run with a team of your friends to enjoy a bonding experience like no other. It is a fun event with lots of music, running, dancing, and color play with non-toxic vibrant paints.

116. Listen to or Watch Inspirational Talks. TED Talks and other inspirational web or television series can be a terrific way to learn new things. If you're not keen on reading, listening to a talk or watching a series is an alternative way to discover ideas and skills.

117. Try a Triathlon. A triathlon combines running, swimming, and biking. There are many different distances, from a short sprint to an all-day triathlon. Like running a race, it is often a lifelong goal. Training with friends can make the challenge much more enjoyable and create a strong bond between you and your peers.

118. Breed Tropical Fish. Breeding tropical fish has become a popular hobby. Join a forum and do your research to find out what types of fish are best suited to your tank and how to breed them properly. You can either keep their colorful offspring as pets or sell them.

119. Try Out a New Sport. There are so many sports to try. You'll be surprised at the number of activities that fit your interests and activity level. Your options are almost endless—from tennis to frisbee golf, from pickleball to badminton. Finding a group or sports center in your area can help teach you how to play and provide you with the necessary equipment.

120. See an Outdoor Movie. An outdoor movie or cinema is a unique way to watch a film. Being outside has plenty of benefits, like exposure to fresh air, grounding yourself with nature, and joining with others outside your home.

121. Challenge Yourself to Summit a Hill or Mountain. You can either travel to complete a bucket list climb, or hike up a hill closer to home. But the bottom line is that inclined walking or hiking is fantastic for your cardiovascular health, muscles, and balance. To start, is there a hill close to your home that you would like to climb?

122. Learn to Surf. Surfing is a challenge, but it isn't too late to learn. Working with a knowledgeable teacher can get you comfortable with the water and your body. Spending time in the ocean is very Zen, reducing anxiety, boosting your mood, and providing you with a sense of inner peace. All this while your body gets a terrific workout!

123. Attend the Olympics. Sometimes there is nothing more motivating than seeing others accomplish physical and mental feats. The Olympics are often the epitome of human skill and would be a fantastic travel destination. If you can't attend in person, an exciting alternative will be to host a watch party with some DIY Olympic-themed games with friends!

124. Watch Wimbledon in Person. Watching a live sporting event builds a sense of camaraderie and community among those in attendance. It can be thrilling to see your favorite athletes or sport in person.

Team spirit can be just the thing to boost your spirits and pull you out of a post-retirement funk.

125. Play Bingo. Yes, bingo is the quintessential retiree game, but for a good reason. There is a lot of careful listening and looking involved with the game. Bingo requires players to have a strong memory, alertness, and fast cognitive processing speeds. Over time, playing bingo might even help to improve your mental agility. Why not organize it at the next gathering with friends and family?

126. Plan and Schedule Your Health Check-Ups. A healthy body and mind is the key to enjoying your retirement. In order to be able to have all your planned adventures and complete your activities, you need to be in the best physical condition you can be. Take time to plan your annual health checkups and schedule them too so you can keep on relishing your retirement!

127. Join a Chess League. Want to give your brain a workout? Try chess. This game of strategy and logic is known for boosting memory, improving problem-solving skills, and encouraging analytical thinking. Engaging your brain with a chess game helps improve its plasticity, keeping you sharp. If you are new to chess, there are several online tutors you can give a try.

128. Go for a Swim. Swimming is a pleasurable physical activity and can be particularly beneficial for retirees. It doesn't place pressure on your joints like other activities. It's great for flexibility, cardio health, and muscle building. Simply being in the water can help lift your spirits. Most community pools have indoor facilities or ladies-only times.

129. Try Biking. Many physical activities can be rough on aging joints, but usually not biking. You can bike outdoors or use a stationary exercise bike to enjoy a good workout without taxing your knees. Biking outdoors with friends can be a fantastic social activity that lets you breathe the fresh air and soak up some vitamin D.

130. Hike. Walking up and down hills will undoubtedly get your blood flowing and heart pumping. This cardio challenge can reduce your risk of stroke, heart disease, high blood pressure, and other ailments. If you want an activity that is more leisurely than running but still challenging, hiking is a great choice. However, I would like to repeat—please consult your physician before trying out any new sports or physical activities.

131. Sign Up for a Water Aerobics Class. We all know that aerobics is fantastic physical activity, and treading water can be good for your cardiovascular health. But did you know that the water pressure in a pool can help circulate your blood better, lowering blood pressure? These benefits, along with quality time with your girlfriends in the water, make water aerobics a perfect retirement activity.

132. Start a Walking Club. In conjunction with how our brain changes to be more receptive to relationships during exercise, gentle physical activity makes walking the ultimate stress reliever when done with other people. Join or start your own walking club, and soon you will be improving your physical health while improving your mental mindset and motivating your group. Going for a walk with others is the perfect opportunity to talk about your feelings and find support.

133. Play Fun Card Games. Almost any card game requires mental skills, such as memory, strategy, and problem-solving. However, the friendly rivalry and flowing conversation that usually accompany a card game are not to be overlooked, often strengthening bonds and deepening relationships.

134. Yoga. Yoga combines physical and mental well-being into one harmonious activity. You can expect to stretch and tone your body while relaxing in a Zen-like state. The repetitive movements are similar to a form of moving meditation, allowing you to recenter yourself and destress. Look around for your local Yoga club or sign up for online Yoga lessons.

135. Join a Golf Club or League. Golf isn't just for guys. It's a great physical activity that naturally encourages conversation and camaraderie. You can golf a few holes with your friends or become a regular at a golf league. Getting outside on those gloriously sunny golf days is also a huge mood booster!

136. Tai Chi. Tai Chi is considered a martial art, but it is non-defensive and self-paced. More used as a form of meditation, this outstanding practice is excellent for seniors. It is gentle, encourages flexibility, and improves mental focus. Tai Chi has also been found to improve sleep, reduce stress, lower blood pressure, decrease joint pain, and increase energy.

137. Host a Board Game Night. Board games aren't just for kids! There are a whole host of games that can be entertaining and mentally exercising. Playing with your friends or family members is beneficial for everyone involved. Making it a regular event can give you something to look forward to weekly or monthly, adding a sense of purpose to your routine.

138. Create a Garden. Gardening is a remarkable skill and good for your body and soul. It can be considered a gentle form of exercise and often requires a few mental strategies for everything, from planning to organizing plant care, with the added bonus of being in touch with nature. When you have beautiful blooms or delicious produce, the sense of pride you'll feel is unbeatable.

139. Create Mood-Based Playlists. Music helps connect us to our emotions. Certain songs can evoke feelings and memories that can affect our moods. Try to create playlists tailored to each of your moods. You can make playlists with soundtracks or songs for when you're feeling joyful and active, a playlist for when you're feeling nostalgic, a playlist for when you need to relax or meditate, a playlist with your childhood favorites, or a playlist with melodies that remind you of when you fell in true love! This can be a great exercise in getting in touch with your feelings.

140. Adopt a Pet from a Rescue Center. Numerous benefits come with adopting a pet, and many of them tend to affect your physical and mental health. When adopting from a rescue center, you are giving a new home to a pet too. Having a pet that requires exercise means that you'll be going for walks more often. The company that a pet can provide is often greatly appreciated by those transitioning into retirement. Additionally, pets typically boost socialization, encouraging you to go to a park, stop and chat with others, or generally be more open to connections.

141. Join a Trivia League. Recalling trivia facts quickly requires a fair amount of focused attention and memory. It's a lovely way to keep your cognitive skills sharp while socializing with others. Consider joining an online league and participating from your home, or play in-person with a local team.

142. Go To Summer Camp. I'm serious! There are summer camps for seniors, and they look absolutely brilliant. They are often themed, having to do with cooking, crafts, or more physically strenuous activities. Regardless of which type of summer camp you choose, it is an incredible opportunity to get away, meet new people, and likely try something you've never done before.

143. Relocate Seasonally. The mental challenge of packing and traveling, plus the light bodily exercise required to load everything up, make seasonal relocation a physical and mental workout! If you have the opportunity to relocate seasonally, either through a second home or a time-share, it can be well worth it. The location change, especially if it boasts warmer weather, can do you loads of good.

144. Practice Self-Massage. Self-massage is excellent for boosting circulation, improving sleep, promoting a good mood, and reducing stress. You can make it part of an entire at-home spa day with some scented candles to relax and mellow down. Use relaxing oils or balms in the comfort of your home. Focus on your emotional health and take some much-needed time for self-care. Scheduling a weekly time slot for this will be soothing and relaxing.

145. Explore a New Diet. Physical health isn't solely based on exercise; a well-rounded diet is significant. Most individuals can benefit from modest changes to their diet, but some may want to do a complete over-haul. Trying a new lifestyle can be fun and exciting. However, to reap the most health benefits, be sure to talk all dietary changes through with your doctor first.

146. Create a Home Gym. You can build your own home gym even if you are on a budget! There are plenty of people, and commercial gyms, selling equipment at a discount. To start, find a safe and comfortable space to work out in your home. You could get yourself some light weights, yoga mats, a towel, and a gym water bottle. Treadmills and exercise bikes are great for a home workout. Some things are even easy to DIY, like a step box. Having these things readily available commonly makes it easier to motivate yourself to work out from the comfort of your home.

147. Join a Gym. If you don't have the space or desire to build your own gym at home, consider joining a gym. With so many options, affordability isn't usually a concern. It's a great way to meet fellow people interested in physical activity and can help keep you accountable.

148. Get Proper Sleep. Easier said than done! If that sounds like you, you might want to consider creating a sleep routine. Your nightly plan can include a bath, relaxing tea or warm milk, reading, or listening to a relaxing sleep meditation. The shift to retirement often means the lack of a schedule, disrupting sleep and leading to insomnia. Consider keeping a sleep journal to discover the areas in which you can improve to achieve a better night's rest.

149. Try a Brain Diet. Did you know that there's such a thing as a MIND diet? This Mediterranean-style diet has been found to slow cognitive decline and reduce the risk of dementia. It can be a fun challenge to try and incorporate the requirements of the MIND diet into your lifestyle. With more fruits, vegetables, and lean protein, you may even find fitness benefits too. As in the case of all diets, please consult your physician first.

150. Practice Memory Tricks. There are many memory tricks and mental games you can regularly engage in to strengthen your brain. Some suggestions are employing the method of loci or creating a memory palace. Little puzzles are quick and enjoyable but can have a significant impact.

151. Go Geocaching. Have you ever heard of geocaching? It is a new sport where individuals hide small trinkets or logs for others to find. The key is that they need to be located using geo-coordinates and a bit of intuition. Most geocaches have clues and take you on lovely paths through nature, local parks, or even downtown. Once you locate the secret treasure, you can leave a small belonging for someone else and add your name to the register!

152. Learn About Health and Nutrition. A health and nutrition course can be valuable and interesting. You'll learn all about nourishing your body and staying active, providing you with a long and happy retirement in which you can comfortably participate in any activity you want.

153. Learn a Different Lifestyle. Have you ever heard of Ayurveda? Do you know what it means to be a Pescatarian or Vegan? There are lots of lifestyles out there focused on well-being. Learning about them and trying to attain the lifestyle can be a fulfilling practice during retirement.

154. Try a Day Unplugged. Sometimes we all need to disconnect for our mental and physical health. Choose a day on which you will try not to watch any television or engage with social media. Promise yourself that you will rely on your electronics as little as possible and stick to it. You can have one of these days as frequently as you like, maybe even once a week! Make sure you notify your dear ones beforehand.

155. Experience Acupuncture. Acupuncture is an ancient tradition in which thin needles are inserted into specific points to stimulate the central nervous system, reduce pain and promote well-being. It is a unique experience that some individuals greatly benefit from.

156. Become a Referee. If you have experience with a certain sport, consider volunteering your time to referee. Youth leagues can be a great way to experience cross-generational bonding. Additionally, you'll get a fair bit of physical activity while you're out on the field too.

157. Get Fitted for Shoes. Comfortable and supportive shoes have never been more important, whether you're walking the dog or going for a bike ride. Now is the time to visit a shoe store and get professionally fitted for a new pair. You'll be glad you did.

158. Train Your Dog. If you have a four-legged friend, try training them! Once you've mastered simple tricks, try doing obstacle courses. Communities often hold competitions in which you run your dog through a circuit. It can be a fun way for you and your pet to get exercise together.

159. Try Disc Golf. Disc golf is an excellent blend of frisbee and golf. You play on a grass course using rules similar to the game of golf. However, you throw small frisbees in an attempt to hit the target, which is a basket down the course. It only requires walking and throwing, making it a gentle exercise.

160. Become an Expert Researcher. Strengthen your knowledge by becoming an expert researcher. You can pick any topic you like and become an authority on the subject. Consider compiling your findings into a book or webpage so others can learn, too.

161. Go Kayaking. Kayaking is an individual sport, though you can kayak with friends. It's a terrific way to get out on a river or lake and experience nature up close. You don't have to kayak white water rapids; it can be fun to gently cruise down a river or along the shore in a calm lake.

162. Try Science Experiments. Science experiments will offer a healthy dose of excitement while testing your problem-solving skills and analytical thinking. It is a great activity to do with your grandkids. Try home kitchen experiments or purchase a complete kit.

163. Go Roller Skating. Roller skating is a whole lot of fun. It can bring back memories of your childhood and is a fabulous bonding activity for you and your friends. It's a great way to get cardio and muscle toning.

164. Sign Up for a Table Tennis Club. Table tennis can provide you with more physical activity than you think, but it's still a low-impact exercise. Think about signing up for a club or league so you can play with like-minded people and have a reason to venture out of the house each week.

165. Play Bocce. Bocce, or bocce ball, is played with balls on a lawn and is similar to bowling. Balls are rolled in an attempt to hit the target, a smaller ball. Played in teams, it's a fantastic way to socialize while getting exercise.

166. Play Horseshoes. Horseshoes offer physical activity while not overtaxing your joints or muscles. You'll enjoy tossing the horseshoes and trying to get a ringer while spending time outdoors in the fresh air. Start your own horseshoe league or challenge your partner to a game one night a week.

167. Describe Your Ideal Day. What would your perfect day look like? Where would you like to go? What would you do? Who would you spend it with? In detail, write down your ideal day. Next, decide what things are feasible and make plans to enjoy them soon!

"Retirement is when you stop living at work and start working at living."

— UNKNOWN

Retirement is the opportune time to focus on your physical and mental health. After all, you're not getting any younger. You should desire to take care of yourself in order to have the most extended retirement possible and enjoy some of the most incredible experiences of your life during that time. Achieving a healthier version of yourself requires a holistic approach. It involves not only devoting time to your body but also to your mind. Work your brain just as you would exercise your muscles. Additionally, take time to rest your mind and center your thoughts like you relax your body after a challenging activity.

Thankfully, it's simple to integrate physical and mental exercise into our everyday lives. Many of these ideas use a combination of mind and body stimulation to nurture our body and soul. Putting in the effort to attain a healthier you will enable you to achieve feats you never thought possible (certainly not during retirement!). If you're ready to take hold of all your post-work years have to offer, you'll love the next chapter, which highlights bucket list activities that are unique, exhilarating, and uncommon.

ACTIVITIES

☐ Plan your schedule for the below activities and add a few more from the above list that you would like to try.

	SUN	MON	TUE	WED	THU	FRI	SAT
Workout							
Yoga							
Meditation							
Swimming							
Brisk Walking							

☐ Which three sports or games would you like to try?

✎...

✎...

✎...

☐ Do you have a pet? If so, what is the name of your pet?

✎...

☐ If you do not have a pet, would you like to get one? If so, which one?

✎...

☐ When is your bedtime?

✎...

☐ Write three good practices you'll add to your bedtime routine for relaxing sleep.

✎...

✎...

✎...

☐ Plan and Schedule Your Health Check-Ups for this year.

✎...

✎...

✎...

☐ Write about your ideal day.

✎...

✎...

✎...

✎...

✎...

✎...

✎...

6

BUILDING YOUR BUCKET LIST OF UNIQUE, UNUSUAL AND FUN IDEAS & CHALLENGES

I've devoted the first few chapters to beneficial, insightful, and healthy ideas that can help keep your mind active and your body young. I wholeheartedly believe that these endeavors are valuable and worthwhile. But sometimes, you need to let loose to counter the destabilizing effects of retirement and discover what your post-work years are genuinely about—*finding you*. These unique and uncommon ideas may just spark your retirement, convincing you that you can accomplish things you never thought possible.

At the very least, they'll expand your mind, provide you with life-enriching experiences, and give you plenty of stories to share with your friends and family.

"You can teach an old dog new tricks, but that old dog has to be willing to learn."

— BRADLEY STAATS

Why is it important to try new things? It comes down to learning. Expanding your knowledge base, yes, but also learning about yourself. We humans do not like feeling vulnerable. Aversion to anything that makes us feel frightened, disoriented, or questioning what we got ourselves into is naturally avoided. But sometimes, all those feelings can be good for us. It's beneficial to push ourselves out of our comfort zones now and again. Doing so blesses us with memorable experiences we will cherish forever.

I'm not saying that you need to sign up for skydiving; we all have different lifestyles and comfort levels. For some, jumping out of a plane might be a walk in the park, especially if your career was being medical helicopter personnel. Though for others, trying ziplining or acro yoga may be far enough off the ground. You get to choose your level of thrill.

You can start by altering experiences you already enjoy. Such as, if you enjoy gardening or taking care of your pets, why not try milking a cow or shaving a sheep, or possibly making your own goat's milk soap from start to finish? It will let you ease into new, unusual activities less intimidatingly. Conversely, you could jump in with both feet and take on the opportunity of a lifetime.

Important Note - please consult your doctor or healthcare professional before trying out any new sports or physical activities, use appropriate safety gear, and use due diligence.

Taking part in brand-new adventures can leave you feeling refreshed, motivated, and excited about what's on the horizon. You'll often walk away with a unique perspective, which can be just what we need when we're stuck in the post-work mindset that retirement means our life is over.

"Nothing is impossible, the word itself says I'm possible!"

— AUDREY HEPBURN

No matter how big or small your bucket list item is, hopefully, it will boost your soul in ways you never thought possible.

168. Join a Flash Mob. Dancing in public can be exhilarating, but doing it on your own can be very intimidating. That's why flash mobs are ideal! By joining a large group of people who dance in public spaces, often with the element of surprise, you won't feel pressure to get all the moves right. Backed by dozens, and sometimes even hundreds of others, you can overcome your fear of public performance.

169. Finish a 1,000 Piece Puzzle. Sure, almost everyone has done a puzzle at some point, but how many people have finished a 1,000-piece puzzle? Working bit by bit on your masterpiece will give you a sense of purpose and motivation. When you finish it, you might be so proud you decide to frame it and hang it!

170. Go to the Horse Races. Horse races are popular events, but they're not something everyone regularly gets to attend. Getting dressed up and viewing the races live is exciting. It helps you feel a great sense of community and like you're a part of something bigger. If you have it in the budget, betting on a racehorse can be a once-in-a-lifetime event (even more so if you come out as a lucky winner). <u>Remember to play wisely and sensibly.</u>

171. Start Your Own Vlog. YouTube is a wealth of information. But did you know the majority of those videos are created by people just like you? You don't have to be a celebrity or a huge company to start your channel. You can vlog and share snippets of your life or teach people a skill. You don't need an expensive camera or equipment to start vlogging. Many successful vloggers use just their smartphones to record and upload videos.

172. Milk a Goat or Cow. Animal lovers will adore this idea. It certainly is a must-try if you've wanted to get closer to nature. When you're done milking, you might be able to use the milk for food or to make a product. In most cases, if you book a farm experience, they'll show you how to milk a cow safely and adequately use whatever is collected.

173. Shear a Sheep. Sheep shearing is another lively experience for animal aficionados. It can be a bit of a workout and a mental challenge convincing yourself to approach a sizable wooly animal. Nevertheless, it's exciting to be sure, and maybe you'll even get to go home with some natural wool!

174. Plan a Theme Park Outing. Taking a trip to a theme or amusement park can be an exciting endeavor! Grab your friends and family and spend a day enjoying each other's company while participating in many great activities. You can ride rides, play games, laugh a lot, and sample interesting food. Additionally, walking all around the park is excellent physical exercise.

175. Try Hula Dancing. Talk about a creative workout! Hula dancing is fantastic and therapeutic. It can make you feel feminine, carefree and make you break a sweat. It's a lovely way to convey emotion through movement and let yourself go with the music. Often, gentle and relaxed movements can be ideal for reducing stress and unwinding.

176. Get Hypnotized. You don't necessarily need to sign up for hypnotherapy (unless you want to); I'm referring to hypnotization for fun. Such as in the scenario when a hypnotist asks for a volunteer at a show or event. Some individuals aren't susceptible to hypnosis, but you'll never know until you try! While you may not be able to remember the occurrence to share any details about it, getting hypnotized isn't something everyone can say they have done!

177. Take an Aerial Yoga Class. Aerial yoga is gentle yoga performed with silks. These silks, or ropes, are suspended from the ceiling and can help you with forming poses. It's a fantastic twist on traditional yoga if you need to shake up your routine. Additionally, it can help relieve pressure on your joints, deepen stretches, and let you enjoy experiencing anti-gravity.

178. Learn a Line Dance. Line dancing has so many benefits it's unlikely you'll want to do it only once! It's the perfect form of aerobic cardio, gentle on the joints and not too fast-paced. Because it's performed in a group with others, it lends itself well to socialization and connecting with others. Line dancing can become part of your weekly routine and will be physically and mentally boosting.

179. Build a House of Cards. Talk about a mental workout; it takes focus and dexterity to build a house of cards, and usually a good number of tries too! It can be a fun challenge to take on with your partner or friends. A card castle or house is a pretty cool accomplishment, so be sure to take a picture to share with your friends and family.

180. Learn and Show Off a Magic Trick. You can take a class or learn a trick on your own. Regardless, once you've mastered it, be sure to show it off! Sleight of hand is one of those things many of us tried to learn as a child, and maybe it's time to invite the magic back into your life. Kids will love it!

181. Sing Karaoke. Stress relief, fear conquering, confidence-boosting... There are plenty of benefits associated with singing karaoke. It isn't just for the younger crowd, either. Karaoke bars are open to everyone, so grab your friends and make a night of it! The release of endorphins you'll experience up on that stage is worth it.

182. Take a Belly Dancing Class. The quickest way to feel young again? Belly dancing! Its fluid movements help you feel feminine, alluring, and proud of your body. It's a beautiful workout that releases tension and produces happy hormones. A pleasant experience, you'll likely walk away from class boasting new friends in addition to new dance moves.

183. Recreate an Old Photo. We all have those cherished photos from our younger years. It might be with your children, your friends, or your partner. Going back to the picture's location and attempting to recreate it with the same poses and attire is a ton of fun. Lots of laughs and unforgettable memories are in store. When you finish, make sure you frame the old and new versions.

184. Try Ax Throwing. Want something slightly daring? Ax throwing has become very popular, often being featured in trendy restaurants. Like darts, it takes mental concentration and good aim. However, it can be slightly more physically challenging; though you'll be having so much fun, you probably won't even notice the physical effort.

185. Take On the Ocean Plastic Innovation Challenge. The Take On the Ocean Plastic Innovation Challenge and those like it ask the world's problem solvers to take on significant challenges. Your ideas could change the outcome for millions of animals and people, impacting the future. Consider devoting your free hours and energy to such a worthwhile and unique task now that you have the time. It can be highly satisfying.

186. Consider Molecular Gastronomy. Have you heard of molecular gastronomy? It's basically food science. This cooking technique focuses on the chemical and physical reactions that happen when food is cooked. It has turned out some fantastic dishes. You can either try your hand in a molecular gastronomy cooking class or simply go out to eat at a molecular gastronomy restaurant. How many people can say they have eaten rainbow foam or disappearing ravioli?

187. Travel Somewhere with Historical Significance. Traveling is one of the top answers when individuals are asked what they plan to do during retirement. Though most probably automatically respond without having a true destination in mind. I encourage you to select a destination with historical significance. It doesn't have to be international; it could be a place in your hometown that you have never been to. Invest some time thoroughly researching unique locations that will renew your spirit and acquaint you with the history of that place.

188. Volunteer to Be a Game Show Contestant. Not many people can claim they were a former game show contestant. Arguably, being on your favorite game show would be an exciting, eye-opening, and possibly lucrative opportunity! In most cases, you may have to fly to where your game show is hosted and sign up to be a live audience member. However, some game shows travel about the country, and with a fair bit of planning, you could be a contestant in your hometown!

189. Go Skydiving or Parasailing. Skydiving is a quintessential bucket list item. For most, jumping out of a plane requires a lot of bravery. Parasailing is equally as bold. For someone who needs this exciting adventure but a safer option can head over to indoor skydiving experience centers. Indoor skydiving simulates the conditions of a true free-fall in a vertical, spacious wind tunnel under professional supervision. Check out the one nearest to you. If you want to overcome fear and see the world from a whole new perspective, maybe it's time to take it to the sky!

190. Fly in a Helicopter. Helicopters are much more agile than airplanes, offering a thrilling ride while giving you a new look at the world around you. Riding in a helicopter is exciting, even more so if you're over a scenic location. It's a fantastic alternative to skydiving or parasailing if you want to overcome your fear of heights, but with added safety measures.

191. Take a Long Scenic Train Ride. It's time to forget about those cramped train or subway rides to work and replace them with a new memory from the rails! Scenic train rides can be a beautiful way to explore the countryside, socialize with others, and learn about one of the oldest methods of travel. Now that you have the time, you'll get to view scenery that you wouldn't be able to see if you were flying, driving, or attempting to hike. A train ride is about the journey, not just the destination.

192. Learn Horse Riding. Did you know horseback riding can benefit your physical and mental health? It's a great stress reliever and will help with your balance, strength, and cognitive fitness. Local stables and equestrian fields commonly offer lessons for all levels of expertise. Sign up for a beginner's lesson if you feel interested. There is value in socializing with others at the stables, connecting with animals, and learning a new skill!

193. Challenge Yourself to Sell Something Handmade by You. It takes courage to sell something that you created yourself. Stepping out of your comfort zone and listing an item you made is excellent for your confidence and self-esteem. Use your talents to sew, knit, cook, or even write something; then, list it for sale online or sell it at a public event such as a farmers market. It could be the beginning of something fun and lucrative!

194. Create Your Own Signature Cocktail or Mock-tail Drink. At one time, all of the classic cocktails were an experiment in mixology. With so many flavors and combinations, there is a world of possibility. Read up on creating new drinks or take a class with your local library, community center, or restaurant. Try making your own recipes for welcome drinks or party drinks. When you've perfected your signature drink recipe, be sure to invite all your friends over for a tasting party.

195. Be a Movie Extra. Did you ever fancy appearing on the silver screen? A quick search online will usually return casting calls for movie extras. Films frequently need extras to simply appear in the background, which requires no or few speaking lines. Though pay isn't typically offered, being a movie extra is a pretty unique adventure to add to your resume. Not many people can claim they have appeared on the silver screen!

196. Learn to Juggle. You probably tried juggling as a child and discovered it was much more challenging than it looks. Now, you have the time to take another stab at it! Once you get it down, you can wow your friends and family, particularly your grandkids. Even if you decide not to show off your talent, juggling is shockingly good for you. It can reportedly boost brain health, improving concentration, coordination, and memory.

197. Try Out Different Wigs or Hair Extensions. Go bold with your hairstyle! Most women covet a particular hairstyle their entire life and are never brave enough to take the leap. Something always stands in the way, like what the employer or friends would think. Retirement is the perfect time to express yourself freely, and it's easy to do so with a wig. You don't need to commit fully, so you can try a different color or style every day of the week!

198. Go Hot-Air Balloon Sailing. Taking a ride in a hot-air balloon is an experience like no other. It is a unique experience and can help change your perspective on things, and it is incredibly peaceful and a wonderful experience you should try at least once!

199. Go on a Safari. Though going on an African Safari is popular, few people can say that they have done it. Get up close and personal with animals you've only seen in movies or museums. It's thrilling and entertaining.

200. Visit the Seven Wonders of the World. If you're a travel fanatic, make a bucket list to visit the World's Seven Wonders. You'll experience things like the Great Wall of China and the Pyramids of Giza. Broaden your horizons, learn about new cultures, and meet new people!

201. Try Go-Karting. You'll feel like a kid again while on the go-kart track! Grab your friends and family and challenge them to a race. It's exhilarating and will undoubtedly test your driving skills with tons of fun.

202. Get a Tattoo. Perhaps you've always wanted a tattoo. Well, now is the time! Work with a talented artist to design the tattoo of your dreams. Do you have a design in mind?

203. Paint a Wall Mural. If you're a talented painter, consider painting an entire mural in your house. It's a beautiful way to showcase your creativity while adding color and style to your home.

204. Visit an Escape Room. Escape rooms are fun and exciting and make for a great bonding experience. You can purchase a kit to set up an escape room mystery at home or visit an escape room center. Those who adore puzzles and challenges will love this idea.

205. Try Making a Duct Tape Dress or Accessory. You might have seen gorgeous prom gowns or accessories made entirely from duct tape on social media. Why not try to make your own clothing or purse? There are plenty of designs and tutorials online; all you need is some tape, scissors, and creativity!

206. Be a Secret Shopper. Being a secret shopper is a great way to get out in your community and earn extra income. Sign up online, and you'll be shopping in no time. Plus, your reviews and feedback can help better the shopping experience for others.

207. Take Up Weather. Become an amateur meteorologist. You can purchase a weather station online or assemble your own. Track the precipitation, wind speeds, and more. There are quite a few forums and groups online where weather aficionados share their findings and ideas.

208. Make Stop Motion Animation. Stop motion animation is pretty cool. You don't need fancy equipment; there are apps you can use with your phone or smart device. Make stop motion animation with yourself as the subject or with figurines, toys, or clay. The options are endless!

209. Try to Break a World Record. There are almost too many world records to count. Some only require time and patience instead of strength or skill. This is an entertaining challenge that can be motivating and provide you with a unique accomplishment when you succeed! Go through the World-Record books to see if anything catches your attention.

210. Learn to Fly a Drone. This is my personal favorite! Drones are increasing in popularity, and it is easy to see why! It can be done only above landscapes without social or security restrictions. These remote-controlled flight apparatuses are easy to learn and fun to fly. Most are equipped with a camera to record aerial video and view it directly from your phone or smart device. You'll wow your friends and family when you show off this skill, I'm sure!

211. Volunteer as a Ride-Along. Occasionally, organizations like police departments or the Department of Natural Resources offer ride-along opportunities. You'll get to spend a shift with an officer, observing what they do while at work. It can be a very thrilling experience and a wonderful way to learn about how these individuals serve your community.

212. Try Cosplay. Cosplay is dressing up as a movie, video, or book character. In most cases, the costumes are made to be as real as possible. The process can involve makeup too. Then, cosplayers get together to show off their talented wardrobe designs at events, birthday parties, meetings, and shows.

213. Get Your Ears Pierced. Get your ears pierced for the first time, or maybe the second or third! If you don't like them, you can always take them out. It can be a fun challenge that will require you to be brave and confident! Did you ever fancy nose piercing?

214. Travel via Merchant Marine. Merchant marine travel is when civilians are offered passage on freight vessels. Often, only a few spots are offered, and there are sometimes requirements you must meet. Nevertheless, it's a unique way to travel and offers a behind-the-scenes look at freight shipping that few get to experience.

215. Learn to Whistle. There are many different ways to whistle, though most of us can only make a single sound of average volume. Learn how to whistle with your fingers or whistle very loud. There are tutorials and videos online that can help you perfect this skill that will stop people in their tracks.

216. Volunteer to Be a Live Model. Art classes at community centers and places of education often need live models. These models volunteer to be sketched or painted by students in the class. Usually, it only requires that you sit still for a while. It's an exciting opportunity if you're looking for a way to interact with the budding artists in your community.

217. Live in Another Country for a Year. Many of us love to travel, but we only briefly experience another country and culture. If you're a travel lover and have the means, try relocating to another country for a year. Immerse yourself in the culture and try a new way of life. Is there another place you have always wanted to relocate to?

218. Take a Holy Land Tour. Visiting the sacred sites of your religion is undoubtedly a bucket list item. It can be a pilgrimage or a tour of what you consider the Holy Land as per your faith or beliefs. It is a humbling experience and can deepen your sense of purpose and belonging while expanding your knowledge and understanding.

219. Learn Ventriloquism. Ventriloquism is a classic hobby that is starting to regain popularity. In this performance, you must create the illusion that your voice comes from a puppet or prop, usually referred to as a "dummy." It's an entertaining talent to practice and even more enjoyable to share with your friends and family.

220. Take Up Palm Reading. Palm reading is practiced worldwide; usually, it is associated with fortune-telling. Whether or not you believe in it, it's a neat trick to share with your friends. You can research and study palmistry online or with books from your library, then practice on yourself and your loved ones.

221. Learn Impersonations. Impersonations take practice, but it is one skill that will delight your friends and family. Research how to do impersonations, then choose a few celebrities or people to impersonate. Practice makes perfect until you've mastered their voice.

222. Go Panning for Gold. Panning for gold is an exhilarating pastime. It will get you outdoors, get you moving, and entertain you with the possibility of finding a golden nugget! If you travel, visiting a place where you can pan for gold should be on your bucket list.

223. Learn How to Organize Senior Tours. Organizing tours is like party planning; it takes organization, communication, and resourcefulness. As a senior tour organizer, you'll meet lots of new people and get to explore exciting places! Consider learning on your own or getting involved with a local company. It might turn out to be an enjoyable way to make extra income.

224. Get Your Pilot's License. For some, flying is a skill they have always dreamed of possessing. Many airfields offer flying lessons for beginners or as advanced as you like. Learning to fly a plane is incredibly rewarding, giving you a strong sense of accomplishment and building your confidence.

225. Build a Miniature Replica with Legos. Legos aren't just for kids. The brand has come out with some very cool and complex sets you can build at home. Most adult Lego sets have over 1,000 pieces and require patience and commitment to building. However, once you've achieved your miniature replica, you'll have a work of art you can proudly display.

"Do one thing every day that scares you."

— ELEANOR ROOSEVELT

It's good to get out of your comfort zone now and again. We spend a lot of time living in complacency. We're often so focused on work and our families that we forget what it is like to do something new, unusual, exciting, and a little scary. New experiences can produce a healthy form of stress and excitement. One that motivates and refreshes you while renewing your focus, creativity, and enthusiasm for life! Trying new things with others also encourages a particular sort of bond, deepening relationships and benefiting us socially. Taking on an adventure is one of the most enjoyable ways to rediscover your identity and work on self-improvement. Small steps outside of our comfort zone now and again bring our lives the ideal balance of certainty and uncertainty.

ACTIVITIES

☐ Select five ideas from the above list you would like to try and include a date you would like to try them by.

✎...

✎...

✎...

✎...

✎...

☐ State five fun adventures you were always afraid to try.

✎...

✎...

✎...

✎...

✎...

☐ List the name of your friends or family members who would be part of your unique adventures and experiences.

✎...

✎...

✎...

✎...

☐ Which is your favorite place(s) in the world that you have always wanted to visit?

✎...

✎...

✎...

✎...

✎...

☐ If you get a tattoo, what design will it be?

✎...

☐ Buy a 1000 pieces puzzle and finish it.

☐ Learn to fly the drone.

☐ Write about your ideal holiday.

✎...

✎...

✎...

✎...

✎...

✎...

✎...

✎...

7

LEARNING NEW SKILLS
WITHOUT PRESSURE

*L*earning is a lifetime pursuit. I wasn't always too keen on that phrase in my school days. I didn't want to *learn*; I wanted to know all that there was to know and finally free myself from my school desk. Somewhere along the way, that changed, and my thirst for knowledge increased. However, as my desire to learn grew, so did the obstacles. A career, a family, a social life—little time was left to learn new skills that didn't benefit my job or my daily household tasks and responsibilities.

Retirement should be considered a blessing when it comes to learning! You have the freedom to learn new skills without pressure. No more do you have to grasp a new concept to be relevant at work or perfect a craft to make your home life easier or more efficient. Learning can be done simply for enjoyment and entertainment.

Sometimes, the number one barrier to learning in retirement is fear. Going back to school in a formal setting, like college or university, can undoubtedly be nerve-wracking for retirees. You will likely be in a cohort with people half your age. However, more and more people over the age of fifty are returning to school and finding immense fulfillment in doing so!

It is not only the trepidation of returning to a college campus that can pose a hurdle. Lots of minor worries may filter through your mind. "What if I'm not good at it?" "What if I'm too old to learn something new?" "What if it is a waste?" Well, one thing is for sure. Learning will never be a waste. You have all the time in the world and virtually nothing to lose. No one is forcing you to pick up this new skill. If you find that it isn't enjoyable, simply move on and try something else!

I think of a man I met by the name of Carson. He was the driver of a jeep that would take us on tour through the desert mountains in the UAE. Carson looked to be in his late fifties and was highly skilled, leading me to believe that he had done this a long time and was nearing the end of an illustrious career. However, much to my surprise, he responded, "Three years," when I asked how long he had been doing this. I wondered, if he had only been doing this for three years, what had he done the other thirty years of his working adult life? Carson answered my unspoken question. He had a degree in engineering and had worked in IT for thirty years, traveling around the world visiting corporations and industries. Then, he retired. Within a few months, he knew that he craved the fast-paced lifestyle he once had, but he wanted to do it on his own terms. He and his wife moved to the middle east, where he decided to learn a new skill—adventure tour guide. Carson relished the challenge it provided him daily. He shared his many life experiences and knowledge with others, and he only took shifts when he wanted to work. Carson didn't fit the profile of the many other tour guides, who were young college students biding their time until something better came along. He also didn't match the profile of a retiree. Yet, there he was, both learning and teaching new things every day, keeping social, staying fit, and regularly enjoying nature. Carson shared his motto for retired life, which I'll never forget:

"Life's a risky proposition; if you want safe, stay home."

— UNKNOWN

Learning something new often requires us to get out of our comfort zone, which can be incredibly good for us now and again. Additionally, learning a new skill can often be a positive counteract to some of the negatives we may encounter during our senior years.

WHY LEARNING NEW SKILLS IS BENEFICIAL EVEN IF YOU'RE ALREADY RETIRED.

Keeps you mentally fit. Learning a new skill helps to keep your neural pathways open. This neuroplasticity, or the ability of the brain to modify connections, keeps our minds healthy and performing optimally. Learning and strengthening neural pathways may help you avoid or delay diseases like Alzheimer's. Maintaining cognitive function can also help prevent dementia and memory loss.

It can be a source of extra income. Learning new skills is excellent for your mental health, but it can also be good for the health of your pocket! If you work to master a skill, you may become good enough to offer your products or services to others. Selling craft items, teaching others about investing, tutoring and childminding or watching kids after school, or being a party planner can all bring in supplemental income.

Improves self-confidence. The personal sense of satisfaction you get from attaining new knowledge and becoming adept at skills can boost your self-esteem. This is especially true if you decide to teach your new skill to someone else. Meeting the challenge of mastering something novel helps to increase your confidence, allowing you to feel erudite.

Encourages socialization. Though you can learn new things at home, most people desire to learn from their peers. You may take a class, enroll in an online workshop, or simply be around others who have something to teach you. These learning methods are excellent for your socialization, encouraging you to be a part of a community and develop relationships with new friends.

Keeps your body active. Not all learning keeps your body active, but most may require at least some physical activity. Learning a new sport will result in you getting some exercise, but even learning to knit can work the muscles of the hands and arms. Keeping physically in shape can help ward off various health problems and issues associated with aging.

Reaffirms your new sense of identity. One of the best parts about retirement is shaping our new identities. Learning new skills and ideas may teach you that you have a creative or athletic side, uncovering a part of your character previously unknown. As you discover more and more things that you are interested in or good at, you learn more about who you are.

Learning new skills can ultimately improve the quality of your life by benefiting your physical and emotional health in multiple ways and allowing you to enjoy the other things in life more fully. Let's now look at a few such options to explore:

226. Learn Adventure Photography. Adventure photography is capturing unique photos outdoors. Often photographers travel to a specific destination or location to capture the landscape or extreme sports, like mountain climbing. Suppose you already know a bit about photography. In that case, adventure photography could be a fun challenge to build upon your existing knowledge.

227. Learn to Drive a Manual Transmission. It is a skill that could have practical benefits in life. However, it's also an exhilarating undertaking that can help keep your brain sharp. We suggest learning from a friend, family member or a professional; it's a great way to boost your confidence and strengthen your abilities.

228. Learn How to Sail. Did you know that there are senior sailing clubs? You can take a few courses or sign up for a summer program. A few places offer a summer residency for both experts and novices where you can become a crew member of a sailboat or tall ship.

229. Learn a Martial Art. There are a variety of martial art practices. You could choose a physically challenging one or a gentler version. Regardless, learning martial arts is a healthy practice for your brain, body, and mental well-being.

230. Learn How to Rustic Camp. Rustic camping, which means more than staying in a motorhome or cabin at a campground overflowing with amenities, is a terrific thing to learn. You'll need to discover how to start a fire, cook over it, purify your water, set up a tent, etc. For outdoor lovers, learning how to camp can be an enjoyable activity that will offer you exploration of many campgrounds, often for less cost than staying in an RV or rental.

231. Learn to Cook a New Cuisine. The possibilities of what you can learn to cook are nearly endless. Many community centers hold cooking classes, and community colleges may offer courses where you can receive a certification at the end of your training. If you prefer to learn on your own, borrow cookbooks from your local library and test out more advanced and unique recipes than your usual fare.

232. Learn Orienteering. Orienteering is the navigation to a specific location only by using a map or a compass. There are orienteering competitions where partners or groups compete to navigate the fastest to each checkpoint. While you may not want to participate in a contest, orienteering is a fun and valuable skill that helps connect you with others, experience the outdoors, and improve your cognitive function.

233. Learn to Make Balloon Animals. Don't overlook the positive side of balloon animals and discredit them as child's play. Using your hands to express yourself through this art form is excellent for your creativity. Once you are successful with a few animals, you can use your skill to benefit others. Try this new skill at your grandchild's birthday party, offer your services to a children's hospital, or simply volunteer at a local charitable event.

234. Learn Professional Knife Skills. One of the most unique and challenging food preparation skills to master is properly using a knife. You can learn how to chop, dice, and julienne. You can watch videos online, read literature, or even attend a course at a culinary institute.

235. Learn to Ballroom Dance. Ballroom dancing is a fantastic way to meet people or deepen the bond between you and your partner. The coordination required to master the steps and movements of ballroom dancing, which often requires a great deal of memory, is a terrific way to boost your neuroplasticity while also getting in a little bit of physical activity.

236. Try Bookbinding. Bookbinding is an ancient skill traditionally done by hand but is completed by machines in modern times. Learning to bind a book the old-fashioned way is a beautiful way to use your hands and show your love for literature. You can learn online or take a class. Perhaps you could bind your own artwork or writings into a gorgeous book!

237. Take a Swing Dancing Class. Swing dancing is making a resurgence. Many high schools and community centers have their own swing dancing teams and competitions. It's excellent exercise and great for your cognition too.

238. Try Glass Painting. Glass painting is a skill that is easy to learn in your home, should you not want to enroll in a class. There are plenty of forms of glass painting, from making fun champagne flutes to creating a faux stained glass window. Your local library should have at least a handful of books and tutorials on this stunning art form. You can also find good video tutorials online.

239. Join a Photography and Photo Editing Course. Thanks to modern technology, we all have photography experience, but how many people have captured once-in-a-lifetime pictures or can edit a photograph from drab to fab? Photography is accessible to everyone, and the skills are easy to learn. Signing up for a travel photography experience can be a unique way to check off multiple bucket list items at once.

240. Learn Fabric Painting. Fabric painting is a versatile skill that can help you refresh your wardrobe, create a one-of-a-kind gift, or even spruce up your home decor. Fabric painting can be done with markers, paints, and even stencils. Visit your local craft store to see if they offer any workshops.

241. Make a Soft Toy. There are many ways to make soft toys, but perhaps one of the easiest is a soft toy-making kit. Available online and in craft stores, these kits provide everything you need to make a lovable stuffed toy. It's the perfect gift for your grandkids or to donate to a children's charity.

242. Learn Nature Photography. Nature photography is a neat skill. It often involves using long-range lenses, strategic planning and preparation, and requires that you get outdoors. You'll often find that it boosts your appreciation of animals and the natural world around you!

243. Learn to Face Paint. How long has it been since you've had your face painted? Remember this enjoyable experience at fairs and the circus? Learning to face paint is fun and creative. It is lovely to share the joy with your loved ones at the next garden party. Once you've mastered the basics, offer your services at local events, churches, birthday parties, and even children's hospitals, where you can bring a smile and excitement to the kids.

244. Learn Archery. Learning archery can help increase your focus, improve your patience, and boost self-confidence! The goal-setting required is excellent for your motivation and personal development; plus, it provides an incredible feeling of self-accomplishment when you hit that bullseye!

245. Learn Dream Interpretation. There are lots of skills you can learn just for fun! Dream interpretation is one of those entertaining skills that you can use on yourself or for amusement with your friends or family. Learning online or from a book is perhaps the easiest, though you could learn directly from a dream expert!

246. Learn to Solve a Rubik's Cube (or get faster). Some people can solve a Rubik's cube in under ten seconds, some can solve it by taking turns with a partner, and even solve it with their feet! Many online videos and tutorials show the basics of solving a

Rubik's cube. There are many options for Rubik's cube solving, and all of them have fantastic brain health benefits.

247. Learn Tie Dyeing. Tie-dyeing is one of those skills most of us tried for fun as children. But did you know that intricate and gorgeous tie-dyeing is an actual art form? Through complex rubber band placement and dyeing techniques, individuals can make breathtaking pieces of artwork. Check out some videos online for inspiration!

248. .Learn Interior Design and Rearrange Your Home. Interior Design is both rewarding and enjoyable. After learning the basics, you can test your new knowledge in your own home. If you feel confident enough in your skills, you could even offer your services at large and help supplement your income.

249. Try Antiquing and Reselling for Profit. Antiquing is undoubtedly a skill. It involves recognizing authentic items versus fake items and assessing what has worth. It can be exhilarating to go into an antique store and make a great find! If you're comfortable parting with your items, try reselling them online for a profit. You could also try out car-trunk or car-boot sales to look for such preloved antique items.

250. Learn to Care for a Pet. If you don't already have a pet, you may want to consider getting one. Animals can be fantastic for our emotional and physical health. Some, like dogs, can promote socialization as well. Learning to care for them is a valuable skill. If you already have a pet, maybe consider getting another type of animal that suits your space and budget. For example, raising a small flock of chickens can have many benefits, such as learning a new skill, being physically active, and providing you with fresh eggs. Why not get a tiny aquarium bowl with some goldfish if you have space limitations?

251. Learn to Be a Sommelier. A sommelier is a wine professional. Sommeliers that work at vineyards or in restaurants go through rigorous training. Still, you could become a local or home sommelier if you choose. There are online classes in addition to in-person courses. When you've completed your training, you could host wine-tasting parties or events and offer your services at community functions.

252. Learn Woodworking. There are many different types of woodworking. Some require extensive tools often found at a woodworking shop, while others, like whittling, demand fewer resources. Whether you want to learn at home or join a workshop, woodworking is a great avenue to express your creativity with your hands. As you become more advanced, you may want to sell your creations or gift them to your friends and family.

253. Learn Glass Blowing. There will be glass manufacturing studios that offer lessons. Working with high temperatures and sometimes heavy equipment is mentally and physically challenging. Try this only alongside a professional person and with proper safety gear. You'll be incredibly proud of your hard work when you've successfully made your first glass piece!

254. Learn to Be a Wedding or Party Planner. Party planning skills are a wonderful thing to have! You will be able to assist your family or friends with their birthdays, events, and weddings. Or, offer your services for a fee to supplement your income. Often it's best to receive some formal or hands-on experience as you will need to organize and coordinate the event, food, decorations, party favors, entertainment, etc. Still, there are also a variety of resources online and at your local library.

255. Learn to Be a Pinterest Expert. Do you love making Pinterest boards? Do you know that Pinterest experts get paid to help companies and individuals manage and create Pinterest content? Many online Pinterest workshops are quick and affordable, allowing you to use your skills for extra money or to create your own unbelievable Pinterest compilations!

256. Learn to Be a Social Media Consultant. Prove wrong those who think seniors and social media don't mix! You may find that you love creating content and following social media trends. Suppose you enjoy this type of activity and are great at getting likes and followers. In that case, you may want to consider how to become a professional social media consultant and get paid for your talents. Learning this skill will keep you fresh, allow you to communicate and interact with others, and it can be lucrative.

257. Learn to Wear Scarves in Various Ways. Who knew there were so many ways to wear scarves? Up your fashion game by learning some beautiful new methods to wear a scarf, whether around your neck, head, shoulders, or even your waist. Look up videos online and have fun trying out various styles!.

258. Learn Cosmetology. Going back to school doesn't necessarily mean returning to college or university. Cosmetology school is also an option! You'll learn things like how to cut and color hair and other beauty treatments. It can be a fantastic choice for those wanting to pursue a second career with their learning.

259. Learn Massage Therapy. Massage therapy is a beneficial practice that can help to relax a person's body and mind. If you're outgoing, massage therapy will introduce you to various people. Should you not want to take the training and get certified, you can learn self-massage techniques to practice at home, improving your well-being.

260. Build a Small Furniture. Furniture building is a beautiful skill. Since furniture is often made of wood, you can join a woodworking shop or take a class. You might learn how to build a table or a chair. These sturdy and gorgeous pieces can be handed down for generations.

261. Learn CPR. CPR is a valuable skill to have. It could save someone's life. Even if you have learned CPR before, taking a refresher course is good. Check out classes at your community center or health clinic, or sign up for an online program.

262. Learn Basic First Aid. There are a lot of components to basic first aid. It's an intriguing challenge that will provide you with a life-saving skill. If you complete the introductory course, you may consider taking an advanced course or even pursuing survival first aid.

263. Learn Aromatherapy. Aromatherapy uses plant extracts and essential oils to help improve your well-being. These oils can be inhaled or applied. It is worthwhile to learn how to properly and safely use them for specific conditions and emotions. You will be able to use your skill on yourself and your friends or family when they're feeling unwell.

264. Make Your Own Paper. The art of papermaking is pretty impressive! It allows you to get very creative with the color and texture of your paper. You only need a few tools and a helpful instructional tutorial. Or sign up for a class at your local center.

265. Try Leathercraft. Leathercraft is a traditional form of art that produces fashionable and functional pieces. You can practice leathercraft at home with simple tools and store-bought leather. Alternatively, local leather shops usually offer weekend classes or courses.

266. Learn Wood Carving. Wood carving can open up a world of possibilities for you. You could carve art pieces, wooden decoy ducks, wall arts, or even a boat. Some people prefer whittling, while others use a chainsaw to make large-scale pieces. It is up to you!

267. Try Travel Toy Photography. Travel toy photography is such a cute hobby, especially if you have grandchildren! All you need to do is select a toy that you have or buy from a store. Then, take it with you on all your adventures, snapping photos of the toy trying new experiences, or taking in the sights. Be sure to send your photos and messages to your grandkids.

268. Learn to Tie Knots. Knot tying is an interesting hobby and an affordable one too. With a bit of rope, you can tie hundreds of knots. Some look beautiful, while others are made to serve a purpose. Should you ever need to tie up a boat to a dock, it's a valuable skill to have.

269. Create a Koi Pond. Your very own Koi pond can be like a personal oasis. Watching these stunning fish is exceedingly relaxing. They have a long lifespan, meaning your initial investment to create their lovely home will undoubtedly pay off, and it can be enjoyed by you and your dear ones.

270. Learn Graphic Design. Graphic design creates visual content or images on your computer or smart device. Various programs allow you to sketch art or make professional-looking logos and signs. If you find that you enjoy and excel at graphic design, you may want to offer your services professionally.

271. Learn How to Tie Flies. Have you ever seen the beautiful and intricate flies used for fly-fishing? Did you know that most of these are tied by hand? Tying flies is a fun art form to practice. You can either use the ties yourself or sell them.

272. Reupholster a Piece of Furniture. If you have a piece of furniture that looks a little drab, consider giving it a second life by reupholstering it! You can give your cushions a completely new look with fabric and sewing skills.

273. Try Decoupage. Decoupage is when you decorate an object by gluing paper designs and cutouts. Usually, a transparent adhesive is used as glue. You can make the paper designs yourself or buy pre-cut stencils. What you can decorate is boundless, including planter pots, frames, vases, boxes, bracelets, or coasters. Personalized items decoupaged with pictures make thoughtful gifts.

274. Learn to Sing. Take singing lessons privately, at a community center, or at your church! Singing is a lovely skill that others can enjoy. Singing has been shown to improve well-being and happiness. Studies have found that people feel more positive after actively singing than listening to music or chatting.

275. Collect Rocks and Learn Geology. Geology rocks! You can collect rocks anywhere and categorize them using rock hunting guides. It's a neat hobby to share with your grandkids, and they'll love looking through your collection.

276. Build a Website. For technology lovers, building a website can be an intriguing challenge. You'll be surprised just how much goes into making the polished websites you're used to seeing online. There are free domains that are excellent for beginners who want to practice their skills.

"Always walk through life as if you have something new to learn, and you will."

— VERNON HOWARD

Learning for enjoyment and entertainment is an entirely different experience than learning a skill for your job, home, or someone else. The lack of pressure helps preserve the purity of learning, allowing you to relish the time spent attaining knowledge or perfecting a skill. Instead of feeling obligated to continue, you can learn new things as you please and let go of anything that doesn't satisfy you. It's the ideal balance of pleasure and purpose, replacing some sense of meaning and engagement you may have lost when you retired. Our curious minds were designed to be lifelong learners—now that you don't have any time constraints, take advantage of this innate passion!

The next chapter will focus on outdoor activities. If you love going out, you will undoubtedly love the ideas.

ACTIVITIES

☐ Name your top three favorite cuisines.

✎...

✎...

✎...

☐ List any five new skills you would like to learn from the above list.

✎...

✎...

✎...

✎...

✎...

☐ Who will get the first soft toy that you make?

✎...

☐ Sign up for First Aid and CPR lessons.

☐ List your top three favorite songs. Do you know the full lyrics?

✎...

✎...

✎...

☐ Which of the below would you like to try this month?

    ☐ Fabric painting
    ☐ Decoupage
    ☐ Glass painting
    ☐ Ten ways to wear a scarf
    ☐ Knife skills
    ☐ Archery
    ☐ Photo editing

8

GETTING OUTDOORS AND ENJOYING NATURE

*D*idn't it always seem like the best weather occurred when you were stuck at work? Gorgeous summer days with bright blue skies, a warm wind, and plenty of sunshine would beckon through the office windows. If you were lucky, you would get to spend part of your lunch break outside enjoying nature. But for the most part, you would get to enjoy only an hour or two of daylight before and after working hours.

Now that you're retired, you can be one of those individuals you used to envy, watching as they leisurely strolled past your window, basking in the fresh air. Nature is fantastic for your soul. It tends to have a healing effect; calming and relaxing.

Did you know there is such a thing as "forest bathing"? Beginning in Japan over three decades ago, scientists realized nature's healing power. As a form of therapy, residents were encouraged to immerse themselves in the natural world around them and reap its physical and mental benefits. Whether you want to sit on your back garden, patio or engage in forest bathing while hiking through the woods, one thing is undeniable— nature can make you happier and calm!

GET OUTDOORS—GET HAPPIER AND HEALTHIER!

Here is how nature can improve your physical health and your emotional well-being.

Lowers Stress and Anxiety. We're often physically active outdoors, which decreases stress. A study found that being active in nature can boost the merits of physical activities. After walking through a forest, participants had good physiological markers like heart rate and blood pressure and reported feelings of increased happiness and lower anxiety.

Decreases Negative Thinking. Being out among the plants and wildlife can change your perspective on life. A Stanford University study reported participants experienced less rumination and negative thinking after taking a walk in the woods. These self-deprecating thoughts are often replaced by self-confidence, peace, and mental clarity.

Lowers Attention Fatigue and Promotes Creativity. Electronic media, including computers, cell phones, and television, constantly bombard us. Too much engagement with technology can lead to burnout, decreasing our cognitive abilities and focus. Spending time outdoors can combat these symptoms, fighting the effects of nature deficit disorder. When you unplug and spend time taking in natural scenery, your brain experiences attention restoration, improving your problem-solving skills, boosting creativity, and encouraging you to have a more meditative mindset.

Encourages Kindness and Generosity. Did you know that gazing at nature's beautiful creations and scenery can lead you to be kinder and more generous? Experts found that participants became increasingly positive after taking in natural scenery and beautiful plants and were more open to helping others. The connection seems to lie in greater feelings of awe when viewing nature, opening ourselves to the idea of a greater good and a bond with our fellow beings, boosting prosocial behaviors.

Boosts Immunity. Many of us know that our immune system can suffer when we spend long periods of time indoors, such as in the winter. Alternatively, getting outdoors is terrific for our health! Individuals who partook in forest bathing showed higher concentrations of white blood cells, your body's defense against germs and illnesses. A trip outdoors might be just what the doctor ordered!

Improves Memory. Nature can improve your short-term memory for the same reason that it promotes creativity. Getting into the wild improves your focus and helps to reset your brain, giving it time to disengage and enter a meditative state. It helps sharpen our attention and ultimately allows us to recall information more easily.

Increases Longevity. We all want to enjoy our retirement as long as possible, and nature might be able to help us with that! A study of women found that those living near parks, forests, and outdoor spaces had lower mortality. It's unclear if this results from air quality, more opportunities to exercise and engage with others, or other awe-inspiring effects of nature. However, the findings were clear that living near flora positively affects our life expectancy.

Let us now look at some ways to spend time with nature and enjoy the outdoors consciously.

"A walk in nature walks the soul back home."

— MARY DAVIS

277. Sleep Under the Stars. Sleeping under the stars will definitely invoke that health-positive feeling of awe. You could sleep outside a tent or camper, cozy up in the bed of a truck or recline inside if you have a moonroof, or even rent a secluded geodesic dome!

278. Experience a Falconry Class. Falconry uses a wild raptor, usually a falcon or hawk, to complete tasks related to hunting. While traditional falconers used to hunt with their birds, the modern-day falconry class usually involves the bird retrieving an object. It's a pretty neat experience, allowing you to get up close and personal with a bird most people only see from afar.

279. Try Bird-Watching. Bird-watching can be done from the comfort of your own home with a bird guide and a good pair of binoculars, but it is pretty enjoyable outdoors too! Bird-watching outside lets you go to the birds instead of waiting for them to come to you. Joining a bird-watching group can help you connect with others while learning the best places to spot feathered friends.

280. Begin Food Composting. Food composting takes your leftover food and turns it into compost that can be used in your garden or flower beds. It reduces waste, enriches the soil for healthy plants, and will require that you make regular trips outside to the composting bin.

281. Consider Beekeeping. Beekeeping is so rewarding! Bees are often friendlier than you may think, and with the right safety outfit and tools, you genuinely don't have to worry about getting stung. You'll enjoy delicious, natural honey for all your efforts in caring for your outdoor, low-maintenance pets! Did you know a single bee can only produce less than one teaspoon of honey in its lifetime! On knowing this, I felt a sense of respect, awe, and admiration for these little hard workers.

282. Organize an Environmental Club. An environmental club's goal is to make others aware of environmental issues impacting our planet. To do so, they commonly get outdoors and participate in eco-friendly events, like park clean-ups. If you don't want to organize your own group, consider joining a local club.

283. Grow Small Flowers or Herbs in Window Boxes. Not everyone has the space to create a large garden. But you may be surprised to learn that a wide variety of flowers and produce can be grown in window boxes, small containers, or hanging baskets. You'll need to venture outdoors to care for them, which is excellent motivation to get into nature daily.

284. Try Bike or Cycle for Short Distance Trips. If you have the ability, consider switching your short-distance trips from a drive in your car to a ride on your bike. It is a terrific physical activity and will help improve your mental health. You'll get plenty of fresh air and sunshine while lowering your stress, boosting your mood, and improving your focus while cycling.

285. Go on a Dolphin Experience. Dolphin experiences allow you to get in the water with a dolphin. You can pet them, ride them, and just be in awe of their extraordinary abilities. Aside from bonding with a dolphin, getting out into the ocean is a beautiful way to see nature and take in ocean scenery. Remember to click a photo!

286. Take a National Park Tour of Your Area. If you're searching for a nature-inspired bucket list, visiting every National Park in your state or region is a fabulous choice! You can take in the sights, go on a walk or a hike, and learn about the area's history. Once you've checked them off your list, you might want to expand your focus, visiting every National Park in your country!

287. Raise Your Own Butterflies. Did you know you can purchase butterfly-raising kits online? They'll contain everything you need, including live caterpillars! You can also assemble all the materials and collect your own caterpillars from outdoors. It's an exciting, cute, and rewarding experience, especially when they emerge from their cocoon and you can release your butterflies into the world!

288. Go Fishing. Fishing isn't always about whether or not you catch anything. It's enjoyable simply to be out on the water, relishing its relaxing rhythm. Fishing is a beautiful way to bond with someone, as you'll likely have plenty of time for conversation.

289. Pick Fruit at an Orchard. Picking fruit can be an excellent way to experience the outdoors and take advantage of a healthy and delicious harvest. It often isn't too physically strenuous, though having the helping hands of friends can be beneficial in more ways than one! Why not pluck some apples or strawberries in your community orchard, if there is one?

290. Make a Plan to Walk Your Pet Daily. We all know that walking is good for us and our pets. However, while we were working, we may not have walked as much as possible. Now that you have the time aim to walk your pet daily. It will become a healthy routine for both of you.

291. Go to Outdoor Displays. Sometimes, museums put on outdoor displays of their work where you can walk through a gallery outside. Metal sculptures and topiaries are some of the most common collections in an outdoor setting. It's a unique way to enjoy art, freed from the confines of four walls.

292. Take a Walking Book Tour. More and more libraries are creating walking book tours in parks and public spaces. Large pages of an illustrated book are printed out and laminated, then affixed to posts. The walking book tour takes you along a path as you read a story.

293. Visit a Nature Center. Have you visited your local nature center? Unlike the zoo, nature centers generally have animals native to your location. You can learn all about flora and fauna typical of where you live and even get the chance to touch and hold some animals.

294. Try Radio-Controlled Toy Aircraft. RC or radio-controlled toys, especially toy aircraft, are exciting and enjoyable. It will get you outside and encourage you to form relationships with others interested in the hobby. You'll love this pleasurable activity, from building to operating your RC vehicles.

295. Go on a Vineyard Tour. What could be better than the outdoors paired with a lovely glass of wine? A wine tour shows you the behind-the-scenes process of how your favorite glass of vino is produced. It's pretty cool to learn about the different types of plants and see the growing process firsthand.

296. Do a Camel Safari. Camel safari is a once-in-a-lifetime experience. You'll see the desert as you travel through the sandy plains on camelback. You can sleep beneath the stars, learn about the culture, and try local food. If a long journey seems too much, some zoos offer short rides and camel encounters that only last a half day.

297. Ride Horses on the Beach. Riding horses can be therapeutic, often referred to as equine therapy when practiced professionally. Arguably, riding horses on the beach can be even more refreshing and uplifting to your soul; the perfect opportunity to connect with nature and a horse.

298. Go Ice Skating. Enjoying the outdoors in the winter can sometimes be a challenge unless you're doing something exciting like ice skating! Whether you're a novice or a natural, you can enjoy this frosty, fun activity. If you are a novice, please skate only under the guidance of a professional skater.

299. Try Snowboarding. Snowboarding might seem scary at first, but it is an exhilarating challenge for the physically fit and adventurous. If you have never snow-boarded or haven't done it in a while, it's a great idea to sign up for lessons with an instructor.

300. Learn to Start a Fire Without Matches. Outdoor skills are valuable and fun to learn. If you were a scout when you were younger, you might have known how to start a fire without matches. Consider relearning this dormant skill and putting it to good use, such as cooking a dish over the fire or rounding up your friends for a campfire.

301. Ride an Elephant. Super Bucket list alert! Riding an elephant is very cool. Some local zoos or traveling circuses may offer the experience. Or, if you wanted to go all out, you could travel to a place like South India, Thailand, or South Africa, where you can also volunteer at an elephant orphanage.

302. Visit a Zoo. Wanting to experience animals without having to leave your state or region? A zoo is a fantastic opportunity to walk outdoors and get closer to nature. Drive-through zoos are a good option for those with limited mobility. Visiting a national Zoo is even better!

303. Visit a Stargazing Park. Stargazing parks are natural areas far away from light pollution where you can look at the constellations with stunning clarity.

Stargazing helps connect you with nature, reframe your place in the world, reduce stress, and spark creativity.

304. Attend an Outdoor Concert. Outdoor concerts are often offered for free, making this a great, budget-friendly activity. Bring a blanket, sit back, and relax. You'll benefit from the fresh air, the bonding experience with your community, and the happiness-inducing effects of live music.

305. Host a Bonfire. Bonfires are lovely in that their ambient glow and warmth provide the best atmosphere for relaxing with friends and family. You can plan an evening party, roasting marshmallows, enjoying hot chocolate, and telling stories. Or, maybe make it a special outdoor date with your partner, cozying up around the fire.

306. Try Scuba Diving. Scuba diving can be a beneficial senior activity in that it keeps the mind sharp and the body healthy while enjoying the underwater scenery. It's necessary to take scuba lessons in order to dive. Once certified, you can scuba in nature, exploring the ocean or a lake.

307. Explore a Cave. Caving or spelunking refers to cave exploration. As long as you choose an accessible and well-marked cave, this can be a terrific activity for the novice or seasoned adventurist. Be sure that you have the proper gear and equipment before setting out on your awe-inspiring trip.

308. Visit a Waterfall. Natural wonders that cause us to feel awestruck can encourage us to be more generous, helpful, and kind. Waterfalls certainly fall under this category. The sight and sounds of a waterfall are beautiful and inspiring. The hike or walk to get to them can also have physical and mental benefits!

309. Go Ziplining. Want to zip through nature like never before? Ziplining is a fun way to explore the treetops and get a bird's-eye view of the wilderness. It's exhilarating and refreshing, speeding through the forest. You should try it at least once!

310. Stay in a Treehouse. If you want to go on a nature retreat, consider renting out a treehouse. Usually considered glamping, these glamorous camping opportunities let you sleep, relax, and dine on the treetops. You'll be closer to birds and animals than ever before and experience a healthy dose of childhood nostalgia.

311. Be a Hometown Tourist. Have you ever been a tourist in your own home town? There may be landmarks and natural features you walk and drive by every day without giving them a second thought. However, when you slow down and take a better look, you might be surprised to discover how beautiful and memorable they indeed are.

312. Become a Dog Walker. If you enjoy the company of friendly canines, becoming a dog walker may be the perfect job for you! You'll get outside, get physical activity, and provide a valuable service for local pets. Plus, it can be an excellent way to make some extra money.

313. Go on a Road Trip. A road trip can be the pathway to taking in some of nature's most incredible sights across the state, region, or country! Strategically plan where to stop and explore, walking through forests, hiking mountains, or strolling the seaside.

314. Try a Wildlife Swamp Tour. Consider a wildlife swamp tour to get in touch with some of nature's more dangerous and exciting residents. These tours take you into the bayou, teaching you about an ancient way of life focused on coexisting with nature.

315. Visit the Vortexes. A vortex is a particular spot on the Earth that is believed to radiate energy. These vortexes, specifically those in Sedona in Arizona, Bali, and Ayers Rock, Australia, are thought to be strong enough to be felt by those standing in them. It is said that their spiritual energy can help individuals reach a more profound meditative state and level of spirituality. Regardless of whether you buy into vortexes or not, the hike to get to them and the connection to the Earth you can feel when you pause and rest on them is unforgettable.

316. Book a Whale Watching Trip. There are a few locations where you can view whale migrations throughout the year. Watching these enormous creatures breach as you look on from a boat is positively breathtaking. The surrounding scenery is often pretty incredible too. When you're finished with your tour, relax on the beach with a cold drink and soak up some vitamin D!

317. Canoe Down a River. Canoeing can be a gentle exercise if you choose a calm river with a good current. While you get in physical activity, you can enjoy the riverbank while spotting wildlife. You may want to consider joining a race with a partner if you're an adept rower. The routine of pre-race workouts on the river will be excellent for your physical and mental health.

318. Try Wildlife Photography. Wildlife photography is the perfect blend of two hobbies—picture taking and outdoor adventuring. You'll often need to venture into the outdoors and stake out your subject to get quality wildlife photos. While you wait for the ideal moment, take time to relax in nature, delighting in the peacefulness of the wild.

319. Cross-Country Skiing. Cross-country skiing is a great low-impact form of physical activity. You'll get to explore the beautiful countryside at a relaxing pace and often without the hustle and bustle of others, as is common in the summer. Find local trails and a friend to go on a cross-country skiing adventure!

320. Fly a Kite. Kite flying is a cool hobby. I'm always amazed at the big, vibrant, and beautiful kites I see outside. Not only will it be fun and entertaining for you, but neighbors and other park-goers will love to watch your kite! It's a great way to socialize and meet members of your community.

321. Be an Amateur Botanist. Botany is the study of plants. An amateur botanist studies the plants around them by cataloging them. You can keep a plant journal, sketching and writing descriptions of the plants you find. Compare them with your guide to see if you can identify them!

322. Go Beachcombing. Beachcombing is physical exercise, outdoor exposure, and a fun hobby all rolled into one! You can collect seashells, sea glass or even pick up trash to make the beach cleaner.

323. Forage for Your Food. Armed with a great guide and careful research, consider foraging for your food. You can make a salad from dandelion leaves, find mushrooms, or pick wild raspberries. Ensure they are safe and edible before putting them in your mouth.

324. Make a Butterfly Garden. A butterfly garden is a garden composed of specific flowers and plants known to attract butterflies. It is an excellent way to help increase threatened butterfly populations, like Monarchs, by offering them an accessible food source. Plus, you'll get a beautiful array of flowers to enjoy.

325. Go Ice Fishing. If you thrive in the cold weather, you might love ice fishing! It involves cutting a hole in the ice and dangling a lure through it. Fish are often slower in the winter, but they can still put up a good fight. Wear appropriate safety gear and try this only alongside a professional. It's an exhilarating adventure that could result in a delicious fish dinner.

326. Target Shooting. Shooting trap and skeet is an excellent workout for your brain. It takes coordination, concentration, focus, and great aim. This hobby is a wonderful way to get outdoors and is best enjoyed with great company!

327. Cross-Breed Roses. Roses are one of the most beautiful parts of a garden. Did you know that they can be cross-bred to create new and exciting blooms? It takes careful cataloging and tools to help cross-pollinate. Like a science experiment in your garden, this activity stimulates the mind and refreshes the soul.

328. Make Maple Syrup. Maple syrup making is an age-old process that produces a delicious treat! If you have the trees, research maple syrup making and gather the necessary tools to tap your forest. Or, you can often find a community syrup class in the spring that details the process and provides hands-on experience.

329. Learn About Homing Pigeons. Homing pigeons are very interesting and historically extremely useful. There may be a homing pigeon group in your area or a local owner who could tell you more about this exciting hobby. If you desire, you can usually purchase your own homing pigeons.

330. Go Noodling. Noodling refers to catching river catfish with your hands. It's pretty exhilarating and requires a fair amount of courage. However, this unique experience will undoubtedly make your bucket list. It's perfect for the outdoor adventurist.

331. Go Fossil Hunting. Did you know that you likely have a fossil site within your town or city? Many places that are dry now were once sea beds and are filled with interesting finds. Search along the beach, go to a known fossil hunting site or look for rocks in your backyard to see what you can find.

332. Ride in a Sleigh. According to the holiday songs, riding in a sleigh used to be common. Nowadays it's a special experience to be had. Share a sleigh ride with your significant other or grab your girlfriends and go for a ride.

333. Learn Survival Skills. Survivalist skills might rarely be used, but they're still useful knowledge to have. Getting outdoors with a group and learning the tactics to survive in adverse situations is intriguing and engaging. It's a wonderful way to boost your knowledge and build new friendships.

334. Build an Igloo. Did you know you can use the tools you have at home to make an igloo? When the temperatures are cold enough, freeze ice in plastic bins about the size of a shoebox. Then, pop them out and begin building. You'll have a neat igloo to show off to your family and friends in a few days.

335. Go Metal Detecting. Metal detecting is fascinating! With a metal detector, you can find all sorts of exciting items. From coins to collector's items, so many things wait beneath the soil. Plus, it is an awesome way to get outdoors and socialize with others in your area.

336. Go Seed Collecting. You can purchase seed collecting kits online or devise your own at home. Then, get out into nature and find unique seeds from vegetables, grains, herbs, or flowers. You can use them to start your own garden year after year or simply preserve them for future generations.

337. Play Putt-Putt. Mini golf, or putt-putt, doesn't require much skill and is a fantastic way to get you and your friends outdoors. You'll have a wonderful time working through the course while engaging in light physical activity and plenty of good conversation.

338. Feed the Ducks. A bag of cracked corn, rice, oats, or chopped lettuce is all you need to feed the ducks at your local pond. It's a great way to reduce food waste while doing something great for the animals in your community. Additionally, activities that involve animals tend to boost socialization and decrease feelings of isolation.

"In every walk with nature, one receives far more than he seeks."

— JOHN MUIR

The mental and physical benefits you can experience when you get outdoors are nearly innumerable. Lower blood pressure, reduced cortisol levels, improved feelings of happiness, better connections with those around us, increased social interaction, and a sharper mind are only a few of nature's positive effects. Seeing the glorious creations all around us relaxes our minds. It offers us a much-needed break from the constant bombardment of today's world.

The peacefulness of the natural world, coupled with fresh air and improved Vitamin D levels, helps boost your immune system, allowing you to fight off illnesses and diseases. Nature can significantly improve your quality of life, and experiencing it is free! All you need to do is step out your front door or enjoy your peaceful back garden. We can be nurtured by nature at any age— now that you have the time, fully take advantage of those days in the sun you once longed for while sitting at your desk.

The next chapter will focus on seniors with limited mobility by providing unique, fun, healthy, and accessible ideas.

ACTIVITIES

☐ List three parks or gardens near to you.

✎...

✎...

✎...

☐ Name your nearest Zoo or National Park. Have you visited it yet?

✎...

✎...

☐ Which of the below would you like to ride?

    ☐ Horse
    ☐ Elephant
    ☐ Camel
    ☐ Dolphin

☐ Plan a Barbeque and Bonfire night for your loved ones. Who all will you invite?

✎...

✎...

✎...

✎...

✎...

✎...

✎...

☐ Write the menu for your ideal Barbeque feast.

Starters:

✎...

✎...

Mains and Sides:

✎...

✎...

✎...

✎...

Dessert:

✎...

✎...

✎...

✎...

Drinks:

✎...

✎...

✎...

✎...

9

FUN ACTIVITIES FOR SENIORS
WITH LIMITED MOBILITY

*T*here are various reasons why a retiree may experience limited mobility. It might be short-term or long-term; due to injury or illness. Regardless of the reason, it's important to remember that limited mobility doesn't impair your ability to enjoy many activities. There are plenty of things you can do, both indoors and outdoors, that are engaging, novel, and beneficial for your well-being.

Focusing on your ability to live a fulfilling and enjoyable life is essential. It may take some creativity, but when you commit to minimizing your mobility's impact on your life and retirement, a world of possibilities will open up.

HOW TO HAVE A POSITIVE MINDSET

Focus on the Positive. Look for the silver lining is an old adage that still holds true. Finding the good in life, no matter how small, can improve your outlook and confidence. Allowing you to experience new things and take on challenges you never thought possible.

Surround Yourself with Positive People. Retirement is a great time to be particularly picky about your circle of friends. As you begin to understand your new identity, surround yourself with people who will encourage and support you and help you to be optimistic.

Be Kind to Yourself. Positive self-talk can go a long way! When you hear your inner voice saying negative things, take a moment to recognize it and identify how this could harm your opinion of yourself and try to turn it around with positive, reaffirming statements. Remember the uplifting Mantras you wrote at the end of chapter two and read them every single morning. We can be our own worst critics, but even small acknowledgments and changes in our thinking can significantly impact our confidence, behaviors, and feelings.

Keep a Gratitude Journal. Starting every day on a positive note is a fantastic way to boost your optimism. Keeping a gratitude journal can help with this daily routine. In the morning, write down a few things or people you are grateful for. Then, throughout the day, find at least one way to express your gratitude, such as telling a friend how much you value them or giving some extra love to your pet.

A new, positive outlook should help reframe your idea of what you can do with your retirement. When considering activities you can participate in with limited mobility, there are two essential things to consider: health and a sense of purpose. Engaging in things that give you a deep understanding of your purpose and a sense of fulfillment is vital. It's easy to feel undervalued and disconnected at the beginning of retirement. These feelings can be perpetuated if you have limited mobility. To beat the retirement blues, you need to find activities that renew your sense of meaning, refresh your spirit, and offer something to look forward to every day. Along with finding fulfillment, paying attention to your health is vital.

There are many ways you can support your health, even with limited mobility. Seated exercises like chair yoga or cardio drumming can strengthen your physical health. Getting outside, connecting with others, and practicing mindfulness will benefit you mentally and emotionally. Taking part in regular exercise for your body and brain allows you to enjoy more of your retirement.

"Optimism. It's not just a mindset, it is behavior."

— LARRY ELDER

339. Take Up a Book Challenge. If you're an avid book reader or want to improve your reading skills, consider trying a book challenge. Most challenges set a goal of a certain number of books per month or even per year. You can find specific challenges that list the books for you, such as all the classics, or read whatever you like to meet the quota.

340. Create a New Baking Recipe. Are you a talented baker? Have you ever thought of creating your recipe and posting it online? Many websites allow submissions from home bakers! You could develop something wholly new or put a few novel twists on a tried and true favorite recipe.

341. Plan a Themed Movie or Web Series Evening. Invite your friends or family over for a themed movie or Web series evening. Have everyone bring snacks or create your own spread. Theme movie or web series evenings, where all the films have to do with a certain topic or theme, are lots of fun! Themes can be comedy, action, fantasy, Sci-Fi, horror, thriller, romance, or it can just be an old nostalgic movie.

342. Try Macramé. Macramé is the technique of knotting cord to create gorgeous textiles. You could make a macramé hanging plant holder, wall art, and even jewelry. It's relatively simple to learn and can be a very calming activity.

343. Take a Seated Strength Course. Most senior clubs and community centers offer low-impact strength courses. A popular one is seated strength, in which participants complete movements with light weights while sitting in a chair. Don't be fooled by the chair; it's a great way to "feel the burn"!

344. Submit a Crossword Puzzle to the Paper. Have you gotten quite good at crosswords? Maybe it is time to create your own crossword? There are online generators, but building one from scratch can be more fun. Once you've completed your puzzle, submit it to a newspaper like the New York Times for a chance to have it featured.

345. Find a New Entertaining TV Series. There is no shortage of engaging television series. Whether you want a documentary or drama, there's likely a program for you. Consider watching (virtually or in-person) with a friend or family member. You can discuss the show each week after the latest episode, providing a regular dose of conversation and connection.

346. Write a Memoir. Writing a book may seem daunting, but writing a memoir shouldn't be scary. You have plenty of experiences and stories to draw from because it is a book about your own life. Many literary professionals can help you create an outline, fill in the blanks, or publish your writing.

347. Join a Book Club. A book club can be the ideal way to meet other like-minded people and get together with them regularly. A book is assigned for everyone to read, then the club meets biweekly or monthly to discuss their thoughts and opinions. There are also several online book clubs you can join and interact with people.

348. Make a List of Things Money Can't Buy. Most people spend a lot of time preparing for retirement financially. However, there are many things in life that money can't buy. Take a moment to list your greatest blessings, whether it is your family and friends, experiences you've had, or your pets. Hopefully, you'll feel uplifted, content, and blessed with your amazing life!

349. Knit a Temperature Blanket. Have you ever heard of temperature blankets? It's a pretty neat knitting idea! First, make a chart, assigning each range of temperatures a specific color. Then, every day for a year knit a line of the color pertaining to the temperature that day. In the end, you'll have a colorful gradient blanket!

350. Listen to an Audiobook. Did you know that audiobooks can elicit a more excellent emotional response than if you were reading the book? Listening to a story can free your mind and immerse you in another world. It's often a fantastic stress reliever. You can listen to your favorite books while doing chores or while relaxing.

351. Try Oil Pastels. Oil pastels are somewhere between a crayon and chalk. With a bit of paint thinner, you can even use them like paint. They're a unique medium that is fun to experiment with, letting you tap into your creative side.

352. Teach a Course Online. If you have knowledge or a skill to share, consider teaching an online course. Several online tutoring websites and programs offer positions and occasionally certifications. It is a terrific way to make extra money, especially for retired educators. Depending on your skills and preferences, you can sign up to teach anything like Math, English, Arts and Crafts, Chess, Knitting, Yoga, etc.

353. Make Flower Arrangements for a Local Church. The art of flower arranging is fun and cheerful. You use artificial or natural flowers and order your supplies for each week online if easier. Consider finding a local church that you can lend your flower arrangements for their weekly services as an act of kindness.

354. Learn Origami. Origami ranges from simple to complex. This ancient art of folding is relaxing, challenging, and an excellent exercise for your mind. It can also help keep the joints in your hands nimble and dexterous.

355. Challenge Yourself to Make a Ship in a Bottle. These beautiful works of art have become rare in modern times, which is why building your own is such a remarkable accomplishment. You can either purchase a kit and follow the instructions or start entirely from scratch, finding materials and building step-by-step from DIY instructions online.

356. Take Up Philosophy. Philosophy is perhaps one of the best ways to stay mentally sharp and improve cognitive function. Studying philosophy boosts your creativity, problem-solving skills, and analytical thinking. Study independently, take an online program, or enroll in a post-secondary course if you're feeling brave!

357. Follow a Podcast Documentary Series. Whether you love Greek mythology or gardening, there is a podcast series out there for you. Podcasts can be more engaging than reading and an exciting way to learn about a new topic or others' thoughts and opinions. Often released once a week or biweekly, you can make it part of your routine to catch up with a friendly voice.

358. Try Chair Yoga. Limited mobility doesn't mean you can't take part in exercise. Chair yoga is relaxing, great for flexibility, and a gentle form of physical activity nearly anyone can participate in. Look for videos online or find a course at your local center.

359. Take a Cardio Drumming Course. If you want something more upbeat than chair yoga, consider cardio drumming. Fast-paced and fun movements set to lively music make these classes incredibly enjoyable. You'll get to work out with like-minded people who will be drumming right alongside you!

360. Learn the Constellations. There are so many ways to learn more about constellations. Doing so can help connect you with nature, give you a more profound sense of meaning, and help to calm your mind. You can use an app for stargazing outdoors or even from your window. Try going to a planetarium, looking through a telescope, or visiting a stargazing park.

361. Start a Collection. Have you ever collected something? Maybe when you were younger? Collecting can serve many purposes; it can be calming, nostalgic, and reminiscent of your childhood, a way to show how much you appreciate an item, or even a method used to learn more about something. While you can purchase collection items, sometimes sourcing them from nature is more fun, like a collection of shells! Other popular items to collect include stamps, coins, cards, hair clips, scarves, perfume bottles, currencies from other countries, and vintage toys.

362. Take a Sketching Course. Drawing can help our brains make new connections and neural pathways, which may help prevent memory illnesses like dementia. It also requires us to use both sides of our brain! Though you can draw independently, taking a sketching course will help you improve your skills and socialize. Consider a still life lesson or a live model session.

363. Try an Adult Coloring Book. Children have long known that coloring is fun! With adult coloring books, you can experience its benefits and pleasantries too. Coloring is calming, meditative, and a simple way to let your creativity flow.

364. Tutor Someone in Your locality. Put your knowledge and experience to good use by tutoring someone.

Place an ad online or in the paper, or perhaps volunteer with a local school or library. You can either tutor for extra income or as a charitable activity. Either way, you're doing something kind for another person!

365. Commission Your Portrait. How incredible would it be to have a professional portrait? You could have an image created of just you, you and your pet, or you and the most special people in your life! If you don't want to sit through a live rendering, some artists can turn your photograph into a drawing or painting.

366. Become an Instagram Influencer. Yes, people over twenty can be Instagram influencers! Many retirees are rocking social media and proving life doesn't stop just because you reach a certain age. It will take creative thinking, commitment, and a willingness to share, but it's certainly a thrilling endeavor!

367. Collect Fine Art. Collecting fine art can be thought of as a skill. It takes knowledge, patience, and a keen eye. You often have to track a piece, research it, and maybe attend an auction. It is rewarding when you finally hold that artistic item in your hands.

368. Update Wikipedia. Many of us don't stop to think about how Wikipedia gets all of its information—it turns out it is from people like you and me! If you know a lot about a particular topic, why not update

Wikipedia? Share your knowledge with the world and help other curious individuals learn something new.

369. Learn Hand Lettering. Hand lettering is a gorgeous art form. It involves drawing letters in a unique font or script instead of simply writing them. After learning the basics, feel free to create. Hand lettering can be done digitally or non-electronically, such as with pen and paper. Hand lettering is commonly applied to signs, allowing you to create custom items for parties and weddings while earning extra income. Have you heard of Calligraphy?

370. Challenge Yourself to Invent a Game. What a tremendous challenge for your brain! It could be a card game, a puzzle, a memory game, or a game where you craft a board, pieces, and all necessary elements. It can be as straightforward or complex as you like; you're the creator! Test it out with your friends and family when it's complete by hosting a game night.

371. Start an Internet Radio Station. Also known as webcasting, hosting an internet radio station is like podcasting. You can start your own radio station and play the music you've created! Or, you could host a talk show. With minimal equipment, sometimes only your smartphone, you could become a radio DJ.

372. Make a Terrarium. A terrarium is a lovely little garden that you build inside a sealed container, like a jar, and then can keep in your home. They're pretty neat in that the miniature garden becomes its own ecosystem once sealed. In most cases, the plants even water themselves via condensation and transpiration. Full of vibrant moss, green plants, and your choice of natural features like stones, they make beautiful home decor items.

373. Learn Makeup. The world of makeup is expansive, from full-face glamour to natural-looking makeup. Suppose you enjoy applying makeup, love being artistic, and aren't afraid to experiment; you might love challenging yourself to create different looks. Once you get comfortable, consider posting a tutorial online or on social media to share your talent with the world.

374. Try Nail Art. Nail art is perfect for art lovers looking to switch up the mediums they use. With your nail as the canvas, you can use a variety of small brushes and tools to paint on nail polish in designs, colors, and even miniature pictures. You could paint your nails solely for you to enjoy or offer your services to others! Consider starting an Instagram account to document all your incredible designs and connect with other nail-art aficionados.

375. Set Up a Mini Hydroponic Garden. A hydroponic garden is a way to grow plants without soil. Online or in gardening stores, you can often find countertop hydroponic garden kits. They come with everything you need to grow delicious herbs, small vegetables like lettuce, and more, right on your kitchen counter. They're pretty easy to maintain and fit neatly on most worktops, making them an enjoyable part of your daily routine.

376. Make Your Own Salts and Scrubs. Bath salts and body scrubs are luxurious and smell fantastic. They're relatively easy to make with ingredients you likely already have around your house. Use them yourself as part of an at-home spa day, or give them as gifts!

377. Write for Your Local Paper. Small local papers sometimes look for guest or volunteer writers. If you love writing, you can offer your services. It's a creative way to get involved with your community by writing stories on local events and networking with your neighbors.

378. Learn Healing Crystals. Healing crystals are crystals used to improve your body's well-being. The thought is that your body reacts differently to various elements found in specific types of crystals. Certain crystals are used for varying conditions. It can be an interesting topic to explore while possibly benefiting your health!

379. Join a Fantasy Sports League. Fantasy sports leagues are becoming quite popular. It's a great way to enjoy your favorite sports teams while also bonding with friends and other like-minded people.

380. Learn Basket Weaving. Basket weaving is an ancient art that is still valuable today. It is usually taught in a class, though you can find many online tutorials. You'll need materials that can be easily sourced from a craft store, and the only tools required are your hands! This practical skill just might help you organize and declutter your home.

381. Build a Fairy Garden. Fairy gardens are fun little displays of creativity. They make lovely gifts as well. You can make a fairy garden out of almost any vessel, using materials you sourced from around your house or store-bought items. Fairy garden kits can also be purchased if you want to keep it simple.

382. Learn Bonsai. Making a bonsai is a beautiful talent. Not all trees can be made into bonsai trees, so be sure to seek guidance from your local gardening store. You'll need patience, creativity, and gentle care to make a tree into a bonsai. Within a few years, you'll have a small, spectacular tree to enjoy inside your home.

383. Play Mancala. Mancala is an ancient game meant to be played by two people—so you'll need to recruit a friend! This simple strategy game is a lot of fun, and its inherent math focus helps to keep your brain sharp. It's one of the oldest known games that is still played today!

384. Try Ham Radio. Ham radio or amateur radio often brings people and electronics together, allowing you to communicate with individuals worldwide. There are many types of radio stations, but using these frequencies often requires learning and practice. Not only is it fun to experiment with, but its particular communication method makes it usable in disasters and emergencies when modern communications are cut off, making it a valuable skill.

385. Learn Morse Code. Learning Morse code can be entertaining and challenging. There are interactive Morse code trainers online you can learn from or join a forum to practice your skills with other people. With careful study, you'll soon be able to write and translate messages.

386. Build a Stringed Instrument. Building a stringed instrument is a fun activity that will result in a beautiful musical instrument. Kits are available online for guitars, violins, and more. Once you have your instrument, take lessons and learn how to play it!

387. Learn Astrology. Astrology is the study of how celestial positions relate to human activity and behavior. There are many different sects of astrology, but most people gravitate towards horoscopes. It's an intriguing topic that can be enjoyable to learn and fun to share with friends.

388. Try Needle Felting. Needle felting can result in some super cute crafts! Such as toys perfect for gifting to your grandkids or donating to the local children's hospital. It isn't hard and is a fantastic activity for beginners. You only need a few simple tools and an online tutorial or instruction book.

389. Press Flowers. Pressing flowers is a traditional hobby that is both pleasurable and beautiful. You can source flowers locally, allowing you to get outdoors and press them in the comfort of your own home. Pressed flowers can then be incorporated into lovely decor pieces or handmade greeting cards for your loved ones.

390. Rock Painting. Rock painting has so many benefits. It helps keep your creative juices flowing as you paint your miniature work of art. And, thanks to the recent trend of leaving painted rocks in public places for others, it's a fun way to get involved in your community and brighten someone's day. You can easily purchase rocks through a gardening shop or opt for a complete kit that contains rocks, paints, and everything you need!

391. Learn Coding. Coding might seem challenging at first, but thanks to fun tools like Raspberry Pi, it's easier to learn than you may think. There are lots of coding projects and tools online, perfect for beginners. More advanced learners could enroll in a course online or through their local college.

"Your present circumstances don't determine where you can go; they merely determine where you start."

— NIDO QUBEIN

Don't let the challenge of limited mobility stop you from enjoying your retirement. You are not alone in your struggles; everyone faces difficulties. Finding a great support system can help you overcome obstacles and deeply appreciate your retired years. A great way to find a support system is to become more involved and try many of these ideas above to help you feel happy, productive, and fulfilled, all while meeting new people.

We are all unique and have something valuable to bring to the table. Remembering this, and keeping a positive mindset during your retirement, can go a long way when it comes to your growth, happiness, and contentment.

The next chapter will focus on activities that you'll find enjoyable if you are a food lover.

ACTIVITIES

☐ Pick three things from the above list that you would like to try.

✎...

✎...

✎...

☐ What are your favorite TV shows?

✎...

✎...

✎...

☐ What's your birthstone or most liked crystal?

✎...

☐ Name three of your favorite art and craft activities.

✎...

✎...

✎...

☐ List five gifts or blessings in your life that money can't buy.

✎...

✎...

✎...

✎...

✎...

10

FUN AND INDULGENT IDEAS FOR FOODIES

Who doesn't love eating delicious food and trying new cuisine? We all have to eat, so why not make it a fun experience! Good food should taste great, nourish our bodies and make us feel great.

Do you know that food can influence how we feel? Some people see food simply as fuel for our bodies, while others view it as a pleasurable activity. Too much of either outlook isn't ideal. Instead, the perfect balance of food for pleasure and health is critical. Appreciating your food for the sustenance it provides but also for the subtle differences in its taste, texture, and appearance. Foodies know all about this.

A foodie is "A person who has an ardent or refined interest in food and beverages. A foodie seeks new food experiences as a hobby rather than simply eating out of convenience or hunger." While most meals may satisfy their nutritional requirements and hunger, they often diversify their culinary masterpieces. They may travel somewhere just to visit a specific restaurant, or order fine ingredients to prepare a challenging recipe at home. They like to try new foods and learn about them, keeping abreast of the latest food trends and what's happening in food culture.

If this sounds like you, here we go with some fabulous foodie ideas!

"Food may be essential as food for the body, but good food is fuel for the soul."

— MALCOLM S. FORBES

---

392. Travel for Food. One common characteristic of foodies is that they'll travel anywhere for a specific restaurant, dish, or chef. The options when traveling for food are nearly endless. Eat a New York bagel in Manhattan or a genuine Italian pizza in Sicily!

393. Experiment with Tea Bags. A benefit of being an adult is that you can play with your food if you desire! One fun way to do this is by experimenting with tea bags. There are plenty of tutorials online, from flying teabag science experiments to teabag art and even at-home spa teabag recipes.

394. Get Fancy with Frosting and Icing. You've probably seen those drool-worthy iced cookies and frosted cupcakes in bakery windows and wondered if you could recreate them at home. Well, now is the time to try! Whip up or buy some icing and work at intricately decorating some beautiful baked goods. Enjoy them yourself, give them as a gift, or donate them to a charitable bake sale.

395. Make Wine by Stomping Grapes. Stomping grapes is an ancient practice. Though modern-day machines have replaced grape stomping, some winemakers believe the traditional method produces a more intense flavor. Decide for yourself by going on a grape stomping tour; popular destinations include Tuscany, Napa Valley, and Provence, France.

396. Catch a Fish and Cook It. Whether deep-sea fishing, fly-fishing or trolling in a lake, there's nothing quite like catching your own fish and eating it. The experience is fun, to be sure, getting out in nature and relaxing on the water. However, the freshness and delicate flavor are unbeatable!

397. Virtual Cooking Class. Virtual cooking classes have become quite popular. You can either sign up for a professional course or follow a YouTube tutorial. Perfect for beginners, seeing the steps and preparation makes it easier to follow the recipe and prepare something incredibly delicious!

398. Hold an Online Happy Hour. Even if your friends and family members are far away, you can still host a happy hour weekly or once a month that will brighten everyone's day and include lots of laughter. All you need is your computer or cellphone and your favorite beverage and snack. Create a virtual meeting and invite your friends, then sit back and enjoy each other's company.

399. Learn Mixology. Mixology is the study or skill of inventing, preparing, and serving mixed drinks or cocktails. You can try your hand at traditional beverages, like a gimlet or create new concoctions. There are plenty of resources to help you, including books, classes, and online tutorials.

400. Start a Cookbook Club. You've heard of a book club where everyone reads the same book and periodically meets to discuss, but have you ever heard of a cookbook club? It is where every member cooks a recipe from the same cookbook, and then they get together to enjoy each other's dish! It's the ideal way for foodies to socialize. If you are interested, send a message to your foodie friends and decide which cookbook you want to start with.

401. Surprise Bake-Along. A bake-along is typically when you follow along with baking a recipe from one of your favorite cooking shows. A surprise bake-along is a bit different in that you'll only be provided the list of ingredients with rough quantities and necessary equipment requirements ahead of time. Then, you'll join the host (usually via an online group or class you sign up for) and follow along to make a surprise confection!

402. Try Making Candy. Traditional candy making is an art form—a very delicious and fun art form. With minimal ingredients and just a few tools, you'll be surprised at all the treats you can make in your kitchen. Share them with your grandkids or give them away on holidays.

403. Learn Latte Art. Latte creations are gorgeous, edible works of art! You can create everything from simple designs to intricate patterns using foam, milk, or cream. The best part is you get to drink your beautiful creation when you're done! It's also a fun skill to show off to your friends and family, perhaps at a brunch you organize and host?

404. Make a Foodie Bucket List or Wish List. Do you have a foodie bucket list? It can include places you want to travel, chefs you desire to meet, and rare delicacies you would like to try. Consider things like tasting durian fruit, eating bitter melon, or hunting for truffles.

405. Create a Signature Dessert. Every food lover has tried their hand at making a variety of desserts, some probably more than once. Pick your favorite recipe and master it to create your signature dessert. Add a unique twist if you desire. Soon, you'll have a dish people are begging you to bring to holiday parties and get-togethers.

406. Shuck an Oyster. You may have tried an oyster, but not many people can say they have shucked one. For the ultimate experience, go on an oyster farm tour. You'll get a behind-the-scenes look at how one of your favorite delicacies is prepared before getting a chance to prepare and taste a fresh oyster.

407. Try Odd Looking Fruits. There's a whole host of odd-looking (and smelling) fruits in the world. But you can't judge a book by its cover; consider doing a taste test of all the strange-looking fruits you can source.

These might include jackfruit, dragon fruit, kiwano, cherimoya, etc.

408. Make Kimchi. Kimchi is a traditional Korean dish made from fermented and salted vegetables. It's tangy and unique and not too tricky to make at home. Prepare your ingredients, add them to a clean dry jar, and then let them ferment following a good recipe you like. In about three to five days, you'll have a delicious dish that's also good for your gut health.

409. Bake Different Types of Bread. Did you know there are more than 100 types of bread globally? And that some predate modern societies? Baking bread is meditative and relaxing and an excellent opportunity to express your creative side.

410. Celebrate a New Food Tradition. Learning about other cultures is a beautiful way to expand your mind and help you to appreciate differences. Food is often a considerable part of the culture; trying a new food tradition is a wonderful way to marry your passion for knowledge with your love of food!

411. Learn to Debone and Fillet a Fish. There is a lot of work that goes into preparing a fish. Deboning and fileting take technique and practice. Learn the method at home with printed or online resources, or take a fishing tour that includes learning how to prepare the day's catch. It's a skill you'll be able to use over and over again.

412. Make Your Own Salad Dressings. Making your own salad dressings can be much healthier than store-bought. What's more, you'll get to experiment with flavors and seasonings to prepare one-of-a-kind creations! You can use all sorts of combinations of oils, various types of vinegar, sauces, mayonnaise, cheese, creams, and whatnot! Consider having your friends taste test your dressings and sharing any winning recipes on a cooking blog or foodie forum.

413. Try a New Veggie Every Week. This is a healthy and tasty challenge that will expand your food horizons. There are a variety of delicious veggies out there and nearly as many preparations. Keep a checklist of what you've tried, checking them off week by week.

414. Make Your Own Ice Cream. What's really exciting about making your own ice cream is the variety of flavors you can choose. Indulgent, sweet, and even savory! You don't need an ice cream maker, though it helps. Many recipes online use everyday household items such as a blender, a mason jar, or even a plastic bag.

415. Try All the Varieties of Rice. You may not have enough time or recipes to try all of them, considering there are more than 40,000 varieties of rice. However, you can certainly have fun tasting all the delicious and unique types, such as jasmine, basmati, black, Arborio, and wild rice.

416. Cook an Entire Meal on the BBQ Challenge. Do you think you could cook an entire meal on the grill, from appetizers to desserts? Invite your friends and family over or plan a special date night in which every part of the meal is cooked on the grill grate.

417. Go Mushroom Hunting. In the spring and into early summer, you can usually find Morel mushrooms, a coveted delicacy. The fall is truffle hunting season. However, nearly year-round, you can find delicious mushrooms in the forest. Just be sure to have a guide handy or take your mushrooms to the nearest mycology association to have your mushrooms identified as safe for consumption before eating any.

418. Grow Your Own Mushrooms. Don't feel like hunting for soft and tasty mushrooms? Consider growing your own at home! You can buy various kits that range from large to small and are tailored for either indoor or outdoor use. Growing fungi is surprisingly easy and can provide you with fresh ingredients year-round.

419. Host an Adult Pizza Party. Think wood-fired pizzas with interesting toppings, served on rustic boards alongside a fancy glass of wine. This describes an adult pizza party where you won't find anyone eating out of a box. Instead, serve elevated pizzas with your favorite adult beverage. Or, host a pizza potluck where everyone brings their own appetizing creation.

420. Gather Honey from a Hive. To do this, you'll need to find a local apiary or sign up for a beekeeping course in your area. They can teach you the basics of beekeeping if you ever want to start a hive in your backyard. You'll likely experience honey extraction and collection at the end of the session, hopefully getting to take home your very own delicious golden honey jar!

421. Try Seaweeds. You may have eaten seaweed in your favorite sushi roll, but did you know that this isn't the only way to dine on this salty delicacy? You can find seaweed snacks, cook up kelp Pad Thai, or make a seaweed wrap. It's a unique sampling experience for the seafood lover.

422. Try Your Hand at Smoke Cooking. You can explore your foodie and outdoor side while grilling and barbequing. Smoke cooking is a trendy outdoor cooking method as well. It is the process of flavoring, browning, cooking, or preserving food by exposing it to smoke from burning or smoldering material, most often wood. Once you've mastered your craft, invite friends and family over to enjoy your creations!

423. Visit a Michelin Star Restaurant. Across the world, there are over two thousand Michelin-star restaurants, meaning it shouldn't be too difficult to find one close by. You can narrow your selection down further by choosing one that serves your favorite cuisine or is prepared by one of your favorite chefs. Should you want an even more exclusive experience, visit a three-star Michelin restaurant, of which there are only 135.

424. Make Pasta from Scratch. Pasta making is an art that yields delicious fresh noodles, perfect for any recipe. There are a surprising number of pasta varieties. However, each one often requires you to prepare the dough with your hands, tenderly rolling and shaping it. Consider following a recipe in a book, joining an online tutorial, or signing up for a pasta-making class.

425. Roll Your Own Sushi. Sushi usually looks just as amazing as it tastes. But getting all those ingredients into a neat roll isn't as easy as it seems. Try your hand at rolling sushi at home or with a class. Most of the ingredients and tools you'll need aren't difficult to source. Once you've mastered the technique, invite your friends over for a sushi party!

426. Make Your Own Cookbook. Are you an expert baker? A home chef that can sauté and flambé appetizers, side dishes, desserts, and main courses? Share your cooking or baking knowledge with the world by assembling your own cookbook. As long as you own the rights to the contents you plan to include, you can publish your own cookbook collection, complete with tips, photos, and delicious recipes.

427. Try Your Hand at Cake Decorating. Cake decorating is a lovely way to express your creative side. It also encourages healthy cognitive function, attention to detail, and hand-eye coordination. You can make everything from sugar flowers to royal icing decorations. The best part is that you don't even need a cake to practice on, as many decorators use mats or flower nails to master their technique before adding it to a confection.

428. Learn to Cook Gourmet Dishes. Many talented chefs helped popularize gourmet cooking at home. You can find their fabulous recipe books or television shows. However, there is now a host of online classes, tutorials, and in-person courses that can teach you how to prepare gourmet recipes. Afterward, use your newfound skills to host a fancy dinner party!

429. Brew Beer at Home. Depending on how involved you want to become with home brewing, you can find small kits online that contain bitters and flavorings to add to liquors, or you can brew beer entirely from scratch. Keep in mind fermenting your own brew can take up to two months, but it is an endeavor that will give you something to look forward to and a sense of purpose!

430. Ferment Your Own Wine. Don't let fancy bottles of wine fool you; you can actually complete this natural process at home! Using fruits to create whatever flavors you like, sugar, yeast, and water, you can make wine from the comfort of your own home. It will take a few tools and around six months, but it is so worth it when you get to pour a glass of your very own country wine for friends and family.

431. Can Your Own Fruits and Vegetables. While you can buy veggies and fruits to can, canning entices gardeners who have a surplus of produce. Canning is an old tradition and a precious skill. After you've canned your goods, you'll have plenty of fresh fruit and veggies to enjoy all year round.

432. Try Eating Only Fruits and Veggies One Day a Week. Do you think you could go an entire day only eating fruits and vegetables? It's a fun challenge coming up with breakfast, lunch, and dinner dishes to prepare that only use fruit and veggies! Plus, your body will receive a healthy dose of vitamins and minerals during your day-long diet.

433. Consider a Cleanse. Foodies love delectable meals, but sometimes a cleanse can make us appreciate food even more. With your doctor's approval, consider going on a whole body cleanse or detox every once in a while. You can try a day of juice cleanse, a fasting day, or a day of raw food diet. But please remember to check with your physician before trying out any diets, diet supplements, cleanse diet programs, weight loss pills, and weight-loss diets.

434. Make Your Own Sausage. With an attachment for your stand mixer, you can make your own sausages. It's an ancient art form that isn't as hard as it sounds. Additionally, you'll get to experiment with flavorings and meat blends. It's the perfect creative challenge for foodies.

435. Go Vegan. People try a vegan lifestyle for a variety of reasons. It can open your mind to an entirely new world of cooking, recipes, and dishes for foodies. You'll learn how to use fresh ingredients and appreciate a different lifestyle. Researchers with a University in California found that vegans have the smallest carbon footprint, generating a 41.7 percent smaller volume of greenhouse gases than meat-eaters.

436. Try Dehydrating. With a dehydrator or certain ovens and air fryers, you can make dehydrated fruits and vegetables, dried spices and seasonings, and even meat jerky. It's a healthy and delicious way to prepare snacks, ingredients, and foods you can enjoy for months after being dehydrated and preserved.

437. Cook Through Your Favorite Cookbook. Many people have at least one cookbook. They probably have their favorite cookbook from which they prepare the same recipes time and time again. Not many people have made every single recipe in a cookbook. It can be a delightful endeavor to test your knowledge and skills while treating you and whoever you invite to dinner to some truly delicious dishes.

438. Make Your Own Sauces and Jams. Making preserves, such as jams, jellies, and sauces is similar to canning. It's a time-honored skill that is still very useful today. Using fruits, juices, and sugars, you can prepare scrumptious jars that you can use yourself or give as gifts to neighbors, friends, and family. Maybe you could even enter your jellies and jams in a taste testing contest or sell them at your farmers market or local garden center!

439. Make Your Own Spice Blends. Have you ever thought about making your own seasoning blends for cooking? Try preparing your own mixes for vegetables, chicken, fish, and more using dried herbs and seasoning. You can try all-purpose blends, Indian-inspired blends, Mediterranean blends, and more! Test it out on friends and family; consider selling your special spice mixtures at farmer's markets or home-goods shows if it's a hit.

440. Dry Your Own Herbs. Do you love tending herbs in the garden? Or, maybe you have your own indoor herb garden. While fresh herbs are delightful, sometimes there is just no way to use them all. Instead of letting them go to waste, consider drying your own herbs by hanging or using a dehydrator. Then, you can preserve them in a jar and use them all year long.

441. Learn to Prepare Charcuterie Boards. Charcuterie boards have become quite popular, and for a good reason. They're both visually appealing and downright delicious! Learn what pairings work well together and how to arrange them on a board artfully. More advanced skills include making roses from deli meats or holiday characters out of cheeses. Invite your girlfriends over to enjoy the spoils of all your practice!

442. Make Your Own Hot Sauce. Have you ever wanted your own signature sauce? Now you have the time to experiment, taste test, and create your perfect mixture. Making a hot sauce is an art, meaning you'll need to do some research. This fun kitchen science experiment is perfect for foodies who want to test their flavor knowledge.

443. Become a Connoisseur. You can become a connoisseur of almost anything, such as whiskey or wine. It involves enjoying the food or beverage and plenty of researching and learning about the production process and complex flavor profiles of the items. You'll be able to impress your friends and family at your next get-together with all your culinary knowledge.

444. Roast Your Own Coffee. Did you know you can roast your own coffee? You'll need green coffee beans to start and some tools like a roasting element. Because you control the roast level, you get to decide the flavor! It's the perfect activity for coffee enthusiasts who want to do more than brew a simple cup every morning.

445. Brew Your Own Hard Cider. Brewing your own hard cider is surprisingly simple. It only requires apple juice, spices, yeast, and a container to brew in. Most of these things are easily found online in a kit or can be purchased at a homebrew shop. In no time, you'll be able to invite your loved ones over to enjoy a glass of your very own homemade hard cider.

446. Turn Average Food into Gourmet Dishes. Have you ever seen online challenges where people have to take average food, like a fast food meal, and turn it into a gourmet dish? It's a challenging but stimulating exercise that will test your food knowledge! Make a fun night out of it by hosting a competition with your partner or your group of friends to see who can turn the food into the most luxurious-looking dish.

447. Eat Your Way Around the World. Adventurous foodies may want to try eating their way around the world from their own homes! Each week try a dish from a different country or culture. Preparing them yourself will teach you exciting new cooking methods and skills, though ordering takeout (or takeaway) is another delicious option.

448. Make Your Own Cheese. You can make your own cheese at home with the proper ingredients and equipment. From soft ricotta to firm cheddars, cheese making can be delicious and exciting. A bit like a science experiment in the kitchen, it can be fun to learn this ancient craft.

"People who love to eat are always the best people."

— JULIA CHILD

Food should be delicious and nutritious. Mindfully engaging in eating great food can boost happiness, decrease stress, and help you to relax. However, it's good to enjoy rich and flavorful meals in moderation. Instead of focusing only on eating, foodies can appreciate other aspects of their relationship with food, including cooking and preparation. You'll get to learn new things, enjoy novel experiences, and bond with others who value cuisine just as much as you do!

ACTIVITIES

☐ Plan your ideal menu for hosting a dinner party for friends.

Starters:

✎...

✎...

✎...

Main:

✎...

✎...

✎...

✎...

✎...

Desserts:

✎...

✎...

✎...

✎...

Drinks:

✎...

✎...

Games, Music Playlists & Entertainment:

✎...

✎...

☐ What are your top three favorite cuisines?

✎...

✎...

✎...

☐ Name five food destinations or restaurants you wish to visit.

✎...

✎...

✎...

✎...

✎...

☐ Which of the below would you make at home?

 ☐ Cakes
 ☐ Cookies
 ☐ Candy
 ☐ Chocolates
 ☐ Ice creams
 ☐ Wine
 ☐ Beer
 ☐ Spice Blend
 ☐ Jams
 ☐ Sauces
 ☐ Hot Sauce
 ☐ Mayonnaise
 ☐ Roasted Coffee Beans
 ☐ Sausage

☐ Cheese
☐ Fresh Pasta
☐ Mushrooms
☐ Bread
☐ Salad Dressing

☐ If you write your own Cookbook, what will you name it?

✎...

☐ Who all will you invite to your Cookbook Club?

✎...

✎...

✎...

✎...

☐ Which Fruits, Herbs, and Vegetables will you grow in your back garden?

✎...

✎...

✎...

✎...

✎...

✎...

✎...

✎...

FREE GIFT

As a Thankyou for Reading the Book so far, please accept my humble gift.
A light hearted entertaining Bonus to make you laugh, think, and have fun!
Download your FREE GIFT Right Here
or Scan the below QR Code

11

GETTING INVOLVED AND GIVING BACK TO THE COMMUNITY

*A*fter years of working, we often feel that our retirement is well deserved, and this is absolutely true. However, it's important not to make your retirement entirely about you. Instead, seek ways in which you can give back to your community. Frequently, retirement can pose a new set of financial challenges that understandably can tighten your budget. But making donations and giving money isn't the only way to help those around you.

Your free time provides you with ample opportunity to give back to your community. The rich life experiences you've had and the knowledge you've gained along the way also present an opportunity to help others. Even learning a new skill can be used for good. There are many ways to help those in need, from formal volunteering opportunities to small random acts of kindness. Giving back to society is good for others and for you as well.

"No act of kindness, no matter how small, is ever wasted."

—AESOP

Givers often experience the most gain in life—in more ways than one. Did you know that volunteering can improve your health, both physically and mentally? Retirees who spend some of their time volunteering and giving back are often happier, less stressed, and feel physically healthier. Here are a few ways in which giving can help you reap positive benefits.

Decreases Feelings of Isolation. Getting out and serving in your community is an excellent way to combat isolation. When you serve alongside others and interact with those around you, you'll receive socialization, strengthen your ties to the community, and form bonds with your neighbors.

Improve Physical Activity Opportunities. Giving back often requires a little bit of physical activity too, whether walking for a cure or cooking meals for others. Getting up and out of your home is a fantastic way to incorporate movement into your day, and that too for a good cause!

Boosts Self-Esteem. When you do something good for someone else, you often feel great! Helping others is a fantastic way to improve your sense of self-worth and raise your self-esteem. When you feel good about what you're doing, you'll feel good about yourself, too.

Promotes Cognitive Function. Volunteering can significantly help increase brain function and strengthen cognitive abilities. This is especially true if you're using your knowledge or skills to give back, such as tutoring or coaching youth sports.

Bridges the Generational Gap. How you serve others today can create generational ripples that help others in the future. Additionally, collaborating in giving your service alongside people of varying ages is a great way to bond with different generations. We can all learn something from one another!

> *"The best portion of a good man's life: his little, name-less, unremembered acts of kindness and love."*
>
> — WILLIAM WORDSWORTH

Want to know how you can help others with your unique abilities and personalities? Check out these ways to give back.

449. Volunteer for a Local Charity. The easiest way to get involved with formal volunteering is to sign up with a local charity. Your community probably has numerous charities and help centers. Pick one or more which is meaningful to you, perhaps somewhere where you believe your talents and skills could be particularly useful.

450. Learn Sign Language. Learning sign language is exciting, good for your brain, and valuable too. Under-standing sign language equips you to assist someone who cannot hear. You'll never know when the need may arise for your valuable skill to be put to use to help someone.

451. Learn Braille. Learning Braille is another good skill when it comes to helping someone in need. You will be able to communicate with the blind if needed, helping them read signs and navigate or even sending them a card or letter! Plus, this will be a tremendous challenge for your brain, improving our neuroplasticity.

452. Support Local Business. Did you know that shopping locally can be an effective way to give back? Supporting small businesses by using their services and shopping at their local stores directly benefits those in your community, compared to established stores and big supermarket chains.

453. List Your Regrets and Resolve Them. There's a phrase that says, in the end we only regret the chances we didn't take, the deeds we didn't do, the things we didn't say. List your regrets, maybe things you did not do or places you didn't go, and decide how you can resolve them. If there isn't any way to resolve them, learning to acknowledge and accept them can be a beneficial endeavor.

454. Shop at Farmers' Markets. Going to your local farmers' market is an excellent way to support your fellow community members. Most vendors live and work locally and rely on your support to keep their business going.

455. Donate to a Food Drive. Food drives are most common around the holidays, but they go on year-round. Some food centers only accept canned goods or shelf-stable items, while others take fresh produce. Consider visiting a local food center to assess what they need most, then figure out if you have anything to donate or if you can go grocery shopping for a donation. Most supermarkets and community centers will have charity food donation boxes.

456. Donate Your Clothes and Unused Items. Now that you're no longer working in an office, you could consider dominating your business attire. Many support organizations that help people get back to work always look for suits and formal wear. Charity clothing stores and programs will take various clothes and home goods. It's a wonderful way to declutter your closet and home while also making a difference in someone's life.

457. Serve on a Local Board. Consider serving on your local government or school board if you want to give back to your community and make a difference. You may have to run and be elected or simply be able to volunteer. Check out school, township, library, charity organizations, citizen's advice bureaus, and other leadership boards.

458. Be a Grant Writer for Charitable Foundations. If you have a writing talent, consider using your skill for good. Small charities and organizations rely on grants to make their mission possible. However, getting a grant often takes a talented grant writer that can be costly to hire. If you have familiarity with grant writing or think you can learn, volunteering your services in this way is a huge help!

459. Volunteer at a Rescue Animal Farm. If you want to get outdoors while connecting with the wildlife that inhabits it, consider volunteering your time at an animal rescue. These farms often take in animals whose owners can no longer afford them or have no use for them. Fun things include feeding and watering the animals, grooming them, and providing them with exercise and socialization.

460. Start a Charity or Trust. For those wanting to give back financially, starting a charity or trust fund can make an impact for generations. You'll want to work with a skilled expert, like a lawyer. But be sure to research your organization and cause first, finding one that means the most to you!

461. Donate Blood. Donating blood is an easy and inexpensive way to make a significant mark on the world, helping save lives, and it has several health benefits. Consult your physician beforehand and ask if you need more information or guidance. Blood donation is significant in helping people undergoing cancer treatment, people with accident injuries, people who require operations and surgeries, and those struggling with blood diseases, among other reasons. Most individuals can donate blood up to six times a year. Many organizations hold blood donation drives, or you can visit a blood donation center in your area.

462. Create a Collection Jar. Creating a collection jar either at home or somewhere in your community (like the senior center) is a fantastic way to make a change in the world. Label your jar with the charity the donations will be going to. Then, wait until it fills up and donate the funds to an organization in need.

463. Coach Youth Sports. If you have skill and knowledge regarding sports, consider donating your time by coaching a youth team. You have many valuable experiences, information, and knowledge that can help the next generation. Also, you'll improve your socialization, boost your physical activity, and experience better moods.

464. Offer Free Tutoring. Were you a teacher before you retired? Or did you excel in a specific topic in school? You can help others by offering free tutoring. Either promote your services online or in the community or consider teaming up with a school or library to see if you can be of assistance, perhaps part-time?

465. Volunteer for Medical Research. Volunteering for medical research can make a difference in someone else's life. There are a plethora of studies you may be able to participate in. It's a great way to give back while also adding a sense of purpose to your days.

466. Knit or Crochet Blankets for Those in Need. Knitting and crocheting are beautiful skills that can be put to good use. You can make blankets, mittens, hats, or scarves for those in need. Donate them to a clothing drive, a homeless shelter, a church, or other community organization. You'll enjoy the relaxing process of creating the item, while others will enjoy the warmth they provide.

467. Make Toys for a Children's Hospital. Do you know how to make toys? Maybe knitting, sewing, crocheting, or even doing woodworking? Check with local children's charity organizations, like hospitals or childcare centers, to see if there is an opportunity to donate homemade toys.

468. Leave Refreshments on a Hot Day. A simple act of kindness is leaving refreshments at a local park or playground during a hot day. Place a disposable cooler with ice and purchased water or nonalcoholic cold drinks on a bench. Leave a sign letting people know they can help themselves to a refreshment!

469. Pay for the Person Behind You in Line. A popular random act of kindness is to pay for the person behind you in line. Most often, this is done at drive-through coffee shops or restaurants. Sometimes your consideration will start a kindness chain with each person passing it on and paying for the individual behind them, and you never know—it will reach someone truly deserving, someone who could really do with a helping hand! —and it all started with a kind thought from your mind!

470. Join Support Forums Online. Offering a listening ear or a shoulder to lean on can be a meaningful way to help others. Aside from supporting your friends and family, you can be proactive with your efforts by joining a support forum or community. If you've faced a specific issue or gone through a problem, offering your guidance and sympathy to others can be greatly appreciated.

471. Compliment Someone. A compliment is a simple and free way to make another person's day! Saying something nice will help lift someone's spirits and encourage them to pass along the kindness.

472. Write a Thank-You Card. You don't need a specific reason to write a thank-you or "thinking of you" card. Take some time to write a nice note to a friend, family member, your doctor or nurse, maybe even the barista who regularly serves you at the café to say thank you and appreciate them. It's a wonderful way to uplift someone.

473. Give an Inspiring Talk. Sharing your knowledge and life experiences is a perfect way for retirees to give back. After all, you have a wealth of information that can help teach and guide younger generations. Consider hosting your own internet radio station or podcast or volunteering to speak at a local event.

474. Teach a Community Class. Do you have a skill you would love to teach to others? Why not reach out to your community center and offer to host a class? Or, you could post a YouTube tutorial or blog about it. There are lots of ways to give back by helping others learn.

475. Work in Your Community Garden. You don't have to have a green thumb to volunteer your time in a community garden. There is often lots to be done! The garden's residents will greatly appreciate all of your hard work when the harvest comes in.

476. Organize a Beach Clean-Up. Sometimes, once-in-a-lifetime experiences aren't about us. They can be about making your mark on the world and doing something positive. Organizing a beach or seaside clean-up effort is fantastic. You'll need to put all your experience and knowledge to work, gathering volunteers and supplies. Once it's complete, you'll feel great knowing that you made a positive difference for so many and made Mother Earth even more beautiful by doing your bit.

477. Volunteer to Build a Home for the needy. Several organizations have made home-building projects volunteering very accessible. Those who would like to contribute can sponsor in cash or kind. There are also all sorts of jobs available for both novice and experienced builders alike.

478. Organize a Community Clean-Up. Whether tidying up a park or the roadside, cleaning up your community is always appreciated. Donating your time to pick up litter helps the environment and makes the community a more pleasant place to live. Plus, you can't beat the physical activity and time outdoors it provides!

479. Certify Your Pet as a Therapy Animal. Sharing your pet with others is a kind and meaningful way to give back. Therapy animals in a hospital or senior center often need to be trained and certified. Putting in the time and effort to work with your pet and then volunteering their services is highly caring and thoughtful.

480. Participate in a Charity Walk or Race. Outdoor lovers and physical activity enthusiasts will love this idea! Give back by walking or running a race for charity. Sometimes part of your sign-up fee will be donated; other times, you can collect sponsorship and donations to raise money. Either way, this charity opportunity can have significant benefits for all involved.

481. Paint a Community Mural. Did you know you can use your artistic talent to give back? A community mural is a large painting that can beautify a space, spread awareness, or simply make people smile. Working with a building owner and community members, you can paint a mural that will help foster a sense of belonging, build togetherness, and promote well-being.

482. Grocery Shop for Someone in Need. If you have a neighbor, friend, or family member who is unwell or with limited mobility, consider asking to assist them with chores and tasks. Often, going to the grocery store can be difficult. Volunteer your time by offering to do their shopping for them.

483. Bake Something for a Neighbor. Express your kindness by baking something and bringing it to your needy neighbor. It's a thoughtful gesture that can make someone feel welcome, strengthen bonds, and show them that you care.

484. Start a Meal Train for Someone in Need. A meal train is often used when someone is going through a significant life change, such as the birth of a child or the passing of a loved one. An organizer enlists the help of community members to sign up for a day on which they'll cook the family a meal and deliver it to their home. Usually, recruiting people is the most challenging part, making this a fantastic opportunity to step up and help.

485. Serve Meals at a Homeless Center. Volunteer your time at a homeless shelter by offering to help cook and serve meals. Giving back to the community and taking care of those in need is an important endeavor that we should uphold no matter our life stage. Additionally, you'll often serve alongside people from different generations, promoting cross-generational bonds and the sharing of wisdom.

486. Virtually Adopt an Animal. Adopting an animal doesn't always mean inviting them to live with you. Plenty of organizations allow you to "adopt" an animal by making regular donations to its care. Endangered animals are often the recipients, though you can also find local programs.

487. Write a Letter to a Soldier. Writing a letter to a soldier is a thoughtful way to show your gratitude and support for people who give up so much for others.

Search online for a letter-writing program or organization as there can and will be strict rules and regulations. However, it's worth it to put a smile on someone else's face!

488. Volunteer at Local Events. Parades, running races, and other local events sometimes need volunteers to help with setup, cleaning, or handing out resources or refreshments. The organizer will greatly appreciate your time and effort while providing you with the chance to meet new people and make their experience more pleasant!

489. Create a Care Package. A care package is a box or basket filled with various items. Depending on who you are giving the package to, these things can be necessities or non-essentials. Care packages are great for soldiers, new moms, new neighbors, or community members in need. You can create one on your own or donate to a formal organization like Operation Gratitude or Operation Shoebox.

490. Offer to Babysit. Offering to babysit for your children or others that you know is often greatly appreciated. It's a thoughtful way to donate your time to parents in need. As a benefit, you'll get to spend time with a younger generation, which can have physical and mental benefits for all involved.

491. Volunteer at a Sustainable Farm. Volunteering at a sustainable farm has significant impacts on your well-being, the well-being of others, and Mother Earth. You can donate a few hours of your time to helping them plant, care for, and harvest produce. Your work with these cooperatives will benefit your local community, often providing food to those in need.

492. Mentor a Child. Mentoring a child is a fantastic way to support a young person. You'll get a chance to teach them essential life skills, listen and show them empathy, and make a generational difference. Many organizations offer mentorship programs for children in foster care or those in need. Contact your local childcare volunteer bureau.

493. Volunteer at an Animal Shelter. If you love animals, consider donating your time to an animal shelter. While this experience likely won't all be fun time with pets, you'll be making a big difference in the lives of needy animals. Animal shelters also need donations, blankets, cleaning supplies, and more in case you cannot spend time for them but would still like to support them.

494. Be a Scout Leader. A boy or girl scout leader is a fantastic way to make a difference in the lives of young people. You can teach them valuable skills and share your wealth of knowledge. It's also great at getting you involved in your community, making a difference through scout projects and group clean-ups.

495. Be a Neighborhood Watch Volunteer. Neighborhoods frequently have groups that help care for the safety of their residents. A neighborhood watch volunteer might work to observe the area at certain times to help prevent crime. Most groups hold various activities. You can create your own by visiting the Neighborhood Watch website.

496. Volunteer to Hold Newborns. Did you know hospitals have what they call "baby cuddlers"? These are groups of people who volunteer to hold newborns. In most cases, these are babies who have to spend long periods in the hospital due to health reasons of the mother or baby. Touch is integral to a baby's development and baby cuddlers can provide this when their parents are not available.

497. Go on a Mission Trip. Your church or an international organization can organize a mission trip. Mission trips can have different goals, be it medical care or supporting people suffering a disaster. Research organizations online and get involved with a group that will use your special talents.

498. Beautify a Gravesite. Cemeteries can be full of headstones whose family members have passed away or cannot tend the site. With the permission of the cemetery, people have begun cleaning and beautifying abandoned headstones. All you really need is water, a sponge, and a brush. It's a thoughtful gesture and a kind way to care for your community.

499. Offer to Be a Chaperone. The hospitals or schools in your community, church groups, or other organizations can often use chaperones. Chaperones in schools are adults who go along on outings to help supervise groups of children. It's a fantastic way to get involved with the younger generation and help a teacher or parent in need! In hospitals, chaperones can assist by helping to protect and enhance the patient's privacy, safety, comfort, and/or dignity during sensitive procedures and examinations with the consent of the patient and doctor.

500. Donate Your Hair. Consider donating your hair to be made into a wig for someone who needs it. Many organizations take the hair of various lengths and conditions. You'll get a fantastic new haircut, and a child or adult experiencing hair loss due to illness will receive a wig.

501. Sign Up to Be an Organ Donor. If you're not already, consider signing up to be an organ donor. You may want to talk to your loved ones before deciding and follow all appropriate guidelines in signing up. Talk to your health professional or physician to gather all the information you'll need. It's a thoughtful way to give a gift to another person after you've passed on; making a difference in their lives and those who know them.

"Do good for others, it will come back in unexpected ways"

— AUTHOR UNKNOWN

---

502. Free Goodwill - Spread the Word! *Helping someone without expecting anything in return brings you greater joy, longer life, and unforeseen financial blessings. Right now, I would like to open your eyes to this exact opportunity by asking this question: Will you be willing to help someone you've never met, even if you may never get credit for it? If yes, please may I request this goodwill gesture on behalf of a lady you don't know and probably never will.*

She is just like you! (or like you were a few days ago), stressed, worried, anxious about what to do with her newfound free time, and looking doubtfully upon her retired life. She is unsure where to go for help, who to reach out to, and what to do....this is where 'you' can help!

I'm a self-published author who wrote this book to reach out to all ladies like my mum Rose, about whom you read/listened to at the start of this book. My humble intention is to reach out to all such lovely ladies to give them hope, joy, and shed light from an insightful perspective on their retired life. This book is the result.

People judge a book not just by its cover but also by the reviews! A review is the most impactful thing you can do to help get the word out. If you have found this book helpful and valuable thus far, would you please take a moment now and leave your review? I promise you it will not cost you any money and will take you less than 60 seconds. Your review can help this book reach more ladies like yourself.

By doing this you'll help -

💜 *more ladies who are worrying about retiring or retirement life.*

💜 *more ladies who are wondering about what to do with their new free time.*

💜 *more ladies to live a more joyful and purpose-driven life.*

💜 *more ladies to have hope that the best is on its way.*

💜 *more ladies to find their new identity and connect with all their likes, dislikes, passions, talents and more.*

All you need to do is, click on the below link or scan the QR code and share your precious feedback.

Please Share Your Feedback On this Link

If you are reading on an e-reader - you can scroll to the bottom of the book and swipe up, and it will prompt a review automatically. You could also go to the web page on which you bought this book, and there will be an option to leave a review.

I thank you sincerely from the bottom of my heart.

"Only by giving are you able to receive more than you already have."

— JIM ROHN

Being generous and giving back during retirement can give you a greater sense of purpose. It can get you out into the community, boosting your socialization and happiness. Volunteering can increase your cognitive and physical health. More importantly, giving back can make a difference in someone else's life. Retirees often have the most opportunity to volunteer their time in ways that can significantly help others. You can also donate your skills, talents, money, and knowledge. Giving back gives us a deep sense of fulfillment, unparalleled by anything else we experience in retirement.

ACTIVITIES

☐ Which of your skills can you use to mentor a child or a younger friend?

✎...

✎...

✎...

□ Name three charity causes that you support or are dear to you for contributing.

✎...

✎...

✎...

□ List five things you'll do to give back to your community, family, or friends from the above list.

✎...

✎...

✎...

✎...

✎...

□ List five people other than your family and friends for whom you'll write a thank you card.

✎...

✎...

✎...

✎...

✎...

☐ List all the things you **don't** want to feel sorry for when 'your-time-is-up' on this Earth. Anything you wished you would have done? Not done? Done differently? Anything you wanted to say to someone? Someone you should apologize to? A task you started but regret about leaving unfinished?

✎...

✎...

✎...

✎...

✎...

✎...

✎...

✎...

✎...

✎...

✎...

✎...

✎...

✎...

☐ List all the things in your life, to this day, that you feel happy and proud about. List your kind deeds and selfless actions. Memorable and fun moments. Heart-warming memories. What are your true achievements?

✎...

✎...

✎...

✎...

✎...

✎...

✎...

✎...

✎...

✎...

✎...

✎...

✎...

✎...

✎...

☐ List the people for whom you have been a blessing. Who all have you helped? You can also list people you can help, someone who deserves a helping hand from you. It doesn't necessarily have to be monetary; it can be a good word, a phone call, a thoughtful meal, sharing something you can spare, or even just a kind, sincere smile!

✎...

✎...

✎...

✎...

✎...

✎...

✎...

✎...

✎...

✎...

✎...

✎...

✎...

RELISH YOUR RETIREMENT

To make a successful transition into retirement, you will need to evaluate your hopes, interests, goals, relationships, mental health, and physical health. For many of us, work provides a sense of purpose and routine. It's essential to keep these things alive when you retire by developing yourself, nurturing your relationships, and pursuing your passions. How you decide to spend your retirement can impact not only you but also your friends, family, and community. Retirees have a wealth of information to share and should be considered valuable resources within their community.

Avoiding isolation, confusion, and depression is vital. The best way to do so is to engage in activities that provide stimulation and socialization. In moderation, that is. There is no need to bog yourself down with busyness; you're retired and earned it! Your hours are yours to do with as you please. What's beautiful about retirement is that it isn't a loss or gain. It is simply a repurposing.

Instead of working to accumulate money, you now get to tap into and enjoy those stores you've been religiously saving.

In the same way, your time, those forty-plus hours a week, can be repurposed and reallocated. Don't think of retirement as your identity or a label. Retirement is a process, a transition. Dwelling on your status as 'retired', can perpetuate feelings of uselessness. When we say something is retired, we often mean it is no longer helpful. That certainly doesn't describe you! You define your retirement, don't let retirement define you!

"Retirement is a blank sheet of paper. It is a chance to redesign your life into something new and different."

— PATRICK FOLEY

This idea can stop some people in their tracks. Especially those who ask, "So, what do you do?" Of course, you could say that you're retired. But that would be a gross inaccuracy. You may be in retirement, but that doesn't fully describe the abundant and fulfilling life you now live, completely unshackled from work. Instead, you can say:

- "I'm someone who has six Saturdays and one Sunday!"
- "Anything except go to work!"
- "Whatever I please. Every day is different; every day is great."
- "Everything I never had time for because I was working."
- "I enjoy my life, every bit of it, and I have the luxury of time without the pressure of work!"
- "Enjoying two of the most beautiful gifts of life - time and freedom!"
- "I do whatever I want, whenever I want, however I want and IF I want!"
- "I sleep, eat, laugh, relax and repeat!"
- "All my Mondays are Bank Holidays!"
- Respond by listing all the exciting, fulfilling, and unique things you get to experience.

If you respond with "I'm retired," people often have one of two responses—envy or pity. Don't give them the chance to pity you because there is no reason they should! If anything, your answer should excite them about their own retirement, renew their hope in the light at the end of the tunnel, and inspire them to start eagerly planning and dreaming about all the things they'll get to do when they retire.

Retirement is both a challenging and exciting proposition. You have the choice to view it as either a blessing or a curse. It's an opportunity to redefine yourself, reignite your passions, and revel in the freedom of spending your days as you see fit. However, you can't stop looking forward to tomorrow to do this. Don't get mired in the past, dwelling on how your hours used to be filled with work. Instead, seize those hours, days, and years and use them to do something fulfilling, enjoyable, and gratifying.

'A NOTE FROM THE AUTHOR'

Dear Reader,

This was a humble attempt to create a book for precious, retired ladies like my mum and ladies looking to retire shortly to help them see retirement from a fresh and joyful perspective rather than a depressing one thought.

I send you my love and hugs wherever in the world you are. I want you to know you are amazing inside out, You are a beautiful soul, You are stronger than you know, You are unique, You are loved and You are enough! Embrace Yourself! Embrace and fall in love with this new chapter in your life! May lots of love, happiness, peace, joy, good fortune, and good health come your way and fill your life.

I hope the ideas and thoughts shared in this book have been fun, helpful, and insightful. If at least a handful of ideas have been of assistance to you or your loved ones, I'll rejoice and feel fulfilled in this mission!

Wishing you awesome days ahead!

Florance.

Please share your valuable feedback and support by leaving us a review.

All you need to do is, click on the below link or scan the QR code and share your precious feedback.

<u>*Please Share Your Feedback On this Link*</u>

If you are reading on an e-reader - you can scroll to the bottom of the book and swipe up, and it will prompt a review automatically. You could also go to the web page on which you bought this book, and there will be an option to leave a review.

SOURCES & CITATION

Anderson, Elizabeth, and Geetha Shivakumar. "Effects of Exercise and Physical Activity on Anxiety." *Frontiers in Psychiatry*, Frontiers Media S.A., 23 Apr. 2013, https://www.ncbi.nlm.nih.gov/pmc/articles/PMC3632802/

Barnett, Inka, et al. "Physical Activity and Transitioning to Retirement: A Systematic Review." *American Journal of Preventive Medicine*, Elsevier Science, Sept. 2012, https://www.ncbi.nlm.nih.gov/pmc/articles/PMC3830178/

Bratman, Gregory N., et al. "The Benefits of Nature Experience: Improved Affect and Cognition." *Landscape*

and Urban Planning, Elsevier, 3 Mar. 2015, https://
www.sciencedirect.com/science/
article/pii/S0169204615000286

Cherian, L, et al. "Mediterranean-Dash Intervention for
Neurodegenerative Delay (Mind) Diet Slows Cognitive
Decline after Stroke." *The Journal of Prevention of
Alzheimer's Disease*, U.S. National Library of Medicine,
2019, https://www.ncbi.nlm.nih.gov/pmc/
articles/PMC7199507/

"The Connection between Creativity & Mental Health."
MindWise, 19 Feb. 2019, https://www.mindwise.org/
blog/mental-health/the-connection-between-
creativity-mental-health/

https://en.wikipedia.org/wiki/
Honey#:~:text=%20of%20honey%20per%20year

The Chosen. https://www.youtube.com/watch?
v=cyisq4ILK4U

"Fight the Climate Crisis by Going Vegan." *PETA*, 20
Aug. 2021, https://www.peta.org/issues/animals-used-
for-food/fight-the-climate-crisis/

"How Being Bilingual Affects the Risk of Alzheimer's."
Mayo Clinic, Mayo Foundation for Medical Education
and Research, 20 Apr. 2019, https://www.mayoclinic.
org/diseases-conditions/alzheimers-disease/expert-
answers/benefits-of-being-bilingual/faq-20058048#:~:
text=Possibly.,the%20onset%20of%
20Alzheimer%27s%20symptoms

"How Being Bilingual Affects the Risk of Alzheimer's."
Mayo Clinic, Mayo Foundation for Medical Education
and Research, 20 Apr. 2019, https://www.mayoclinic.
org/diseases-conditions/alzheimers-disease/expert-
answers/benefits-of-being-bilingual/faq-20058048#:~:
text=Possibly.,the%20onset%20of%
20Alzheimer%27s%20symptoms

Kao, Josie. "Why Friendships Are Even More Important
in Retirement." *The Globe and Mail*, 5 Jan. 2022, https://
www.theglobeandmail.com/life/article-why-
friendships-are-even-more-important-in-retirement/

Kenneth M. Langa, MD. "Prevalence of Dementia in the
United States in 2000 and 2012." *JAMA Internal
Medicine*, JAMA Network, 1 Jan. 2017, https://
jamanetwork.com/journals/jamainternalmedicine/
article-abstract/2587084

Langhammer, Birgitta, et al. "The Importance of Physical Activity Exercise among Older People." *BioMed Research International*, Hindawi, 5 Dec. 2018, https://www.ncbi.nlm.nih.gov/pmc/articles/PMC6304477/

Lee, Juyoung, et al. "Influence of Forest Therapy on Cardiovascular Relaxation in Young Adults." *Evidence-Based Complementary and Alternative Medicine*, Hindawi, 10 Feb. 2014, https://www.hindawi.com/journals/ecam/2014/834360/

The Relationship between the ... - Wiley Online Library. https://onlinelibrary.wiley.com/doi/10.1002/gps.5085

Richards, Ruth, and Mihaly Csikszentmihalyi. *Everyday Creativity and New Views of Human Nature: Psychological, Social, and Spiritual Perspectives.* American Psychological Association, 2009.

Singh, Maanvi. "If You Feel Thankful, Write It down. It's Good for Your Health." *NPR*, NPR, 24 Dec. 2018, https://www.npr.org/sections/health-shots/2018/12/24/678232331/if-you-feel-thankful-write-it-down-its-good-for-your-health#:~:text=Tiny%20Desk%20Contest-,Gratitude%20Journaling%20Is%20Good%20For%20Your%20Mental%20Health%20And%20Maybe,the%20risk%20of%20heart%20disease

So Byunghun, et al. "Exercise-Induced Myokines in Health and Metabolic Diseases." *Integrative Medicine Research*, Elsevier, 5 Oct. 2014, https://www.sciencedirect.com/science/article/pii/S2213422014000705

"Why Try Tai Chi?" *Mayo Clinic*, Mayo Foundation for Medical Education and Research, 26 Feb. 2021, https://www.mayoclinic.org/healthy-lifestyle/stress-management/in-depth/tai-chi/art-20045184

Yeung, Jerf W K, et al. "Volunteering and Health Benefits in General Adults: Cumulative Effects and Forms." *BMC Public Health*, BioMed Central, 11 July 2017, https://www.ncbi.nlm.nih.gov/pmc/articles/PMC5504679/

Health benefits of donating blood: https://www.stmaryskc.com/news/2017/january/health-benefits-of-donating-blood/

Choir singing improves health, happiness https://www.ox.ac.uk/research/choir-singing-improves-health-happiness-%E2%80%93-and-perfect-icebreaker

The best Cricut machines https://www.creativebloq.com/buying-guides/best-cricut-machines

The relationship between the frequency of number-puzzle use and baseline cognitive function in a large online sample of adults aged 50 and over https://onlinelibrary.wiley.com/doi/abs/10.1002/gps.5085

Made in the USA
Columbia, SC
15 July 2023

c3046d81-5267-46f8-977d-2dad7c41e7dfR01